I Had Dreams of a Happy House Now I'm a FORMER SPOUSE

Larry Lipiec,
B.A., LL.B., ATPL

The Financial, Legal and Practical Realities of:
Dating, Engagement, Marriage, Divorce and Re-Marriage

Continental Atlantic Publications Inc.

Printed in Canada

ISBN — 0-9683513-7-9

Published by Continental Atlantic Publications Inc.

American inquiries can be made care of:
Continental Atlantic Publications Inc.
PMB # 106-229
4200 Wisconsin Avenue N.W.,
Washington DC
20016-2143

Canadian inquiries can be made care of:
Continental Atlantic Publications Inc.
7951 Yonge St.
Thornhill, Ontario
Canada
L3T 2C4

Telephone Toll Free: (USA & Canada) 1-877-439-3999
www.helpmelarry.com

DISCLAIMER: The discussion in this book should not be considered legal or financial advice. Legal and financial advice can only be obtained from a professional in your
jurisdiction. Please consult your own professional advisor with respect to any steps you
wish to carry out as a result of reading this book. The laws governing the various topics,
which are discussed in this book, will vary depending upon where you live or where your
assets are located.

a word about the author

Larry Lipiec is a lawyer and a professional pilot.

Most importantly, Larry is the father of two wonderful daughters.

Everyday his law practice puts him in contact with people from all walks of life.

He meets people who are planning to marry; people who are married (some happy, some not); people who are contemplating separation and those who are separated or divorced (some amicable, some bitter); he also meets many people who are thinking about re marriage or have re-married (some many times).

In his book he shares what he has learned from behind the closed door of his office. His law practice has been featured on numerous television and radio shows and has been the focus of many newspaper and magazine articles. He is a frequent speaker at seminars and is the author of magazine and newspaper articles.

This book is dedicated to my two loving daughters and to all children who live through the heartbreak and pain of separation and divorce.

foreword

This is a revised edition of my book. I knew from the response I received from the first printing that I had hit a nerve.

I would like to thank all those who took the time to contact me. Special thanks to those who visited my website www.helpmelarry.com and shared their own relationship experience or experiences. The response was so overwhelming I had to include many of the most memorable emails and letters in this edition. You'll find them in the last chapter.

In order to ensure privacy and confidentiality any reference to names and places have been altered.

Many of you asked for more information. In response, I added a section entitled "Your Tips," My Legal/Financial Tips and broke them down into the following categories:

- Before Marriage
- During Marriage
- Marriage breakdown/divorce
- Second and subsequent marriages

I hope you enjoy this latest version. Most importantly, my hope is that this book touches your heart and mind when it comes to relationships.

Table of Contents

Introduction

It was a beautiful day. They exchanged vows with love, enthusiasm and optimism in their hearts. The ceremony was flawless and the reception was ideal. It was when the groom was asked to say a few words about his new bride that my mind drifted back to May 23, 1987. His opening words sent a shiver down my spine. He began his speech by emphasizing how lucky he was for having married such a beautiful woman.

May 23, 1987 was my wedding day. It was also a beautiful day. We exchanged vows and promises with enthusiasm and optimism in our hearts. I will never forget the beam of pride emanating from mother and father's faces and my new parents' faces as they watched my bride and me walk down the aisle. My friends, family and other guests congratulated me and commented how lucky I was for having married such a beautiful woman. When I was asked to say a few words, I got up and glanced lovingly at my new bride in her white satin dress. I looked down the head table and saw our families' smiling faces. I looked at the guests and spoke of how fortunate I was to have married such a beautiful lady.

It's many years later and I am single again. "That beautiful woman" and "this lucky guy" are separated. She's now my former spouse. I can't believe it happened to me.

Let me tell you … separation is nothing short of devastating. At first, I was shocked and felt bitter pain in my heart. I telephoned my best friends and cried. I cried for my children. I cried for my parents and cried for my memories. The memories of the happy times. The wedding day. Our honeymoon. Searching for our first home. Holding my wife's hand in the delivery room. Witnessing the birth of my daughters. Seeing my parents hug my children. Birthday parties. The family portrait. First day of school. Shoveling snow together. Hearing my children tell us endlessly how much they love mommy and daddy.

Suddenly I lost my family. I was alone. It was as if a part of me had been torn away.

How could this happen to me? I thought marriage was forever. All of a sudden we became a statistic.

It was not until my ex-wife uttered those infamous words — "I don't love you any more and I want a separation" that I realized it takes two people to marry, but only one to end a marriage.

It has been several years since that day. Now I have a totally different life. I don't live in a house anymore. I live in a basement apartment. My ex-wife and my kids live in our old house in a different city. My ex-wife has sole custody of our children and I am only entitled to visits. I speak to them periodically on the phone. I rarely speak to my ex-wife. I never see my in-laws. I don't know who my children's friends are. I don't know their teachers' names. What bedtime stories they like. I have never been invited to their birthday parties. I don't know what they do in their spare time. We no longer take walks after dinner or take trips to the park. Some people say I am nothing more than an "uncle" to my kids. Boy was I ever lucky!

Since my separation, I have had a great deal of time to think about what went wrong to that wonderful couple who had so much to look forward to on their wedding day. I know that I am not alone.

As a lawyer, I meet many people who are either separated or divorced. At one time in their lives these people were one half of a happy couple just like me. I also have the opportunity to meet happily married couples, many of whom have been married for a very long time. I also meet many "second time arounders" who have gone through the pain of separation and divorce and chose to re-marry.

After my separation, I began to speak to my clients about their life situations. I questioned those who had separated or divorced about what went wrong in their marriage. We also discussed what they would have done differently and what they should have done. I also questioned the happily married clients to learn what they did to make their marriages a success. Finally, I asked the "second time arounders" what advice they could offer to those thinking about re-marriage.

Over the last while, I have learned a great deal from my own personal experience and from discussions with my clients. If only I had the benefit of these insights in my younger days. So many people make the jump to marriage without really understanding what marriage is all about. Let's face it, before you can legally drive, you take a course and must pass a test. Before I learned to fly an airplane, I had to take flying lessons. Before I became a lawyer, I had to complete high school, get an undergraduate degree, pass law school and then pass the bar. Yet to get married, all I had to do was say, "I do."

One of my clients inspired me to write this book. Her 20-year-old daughter was talking about marrying the first boy she had ever dated and believes marriage is like a fairy tale. My client and I know better. We've been there. It is my hope this book will help shed some light on the realities of dating, going steady, engagement, marriage, separation, divorce and re-marriage, so you won't have to say — "If only I had known."

Meeting and Dating
(Why settle for the first person who comes along?)

I can remember my life as a teenager. It seems like yesterday. Life was great. With the exception of studying, writing exams and term papers, I had few worries. There was a roof over my head. Food was always on the table. My laundry was always done. There were no expenses other than "fun"  expenses. My only concerns were related to what to do on the weekend and meeting women. Meeting a girl seemed to be the biggest challenge.

I'll never forget my first date. It was based on a challenge. A friend of mine dared me to ask Lizanne (one of the most beautiful young women in high school) to go out with me. Well, I finally got enough nerve and asked her out. I could not believe it when she accepted. I remember being lost for words. I didn't really know Lizanne. I didn't know what her interests were or even what food she liked. What I was sure about was that she was "a beauty" and I had won the bet.

Looking back on most of my dates, including my dates with the person I married, I can honestly say they all centered upon good times and physical attractions. A date was anything but reality. Let's face it, when you're on a date you're always on your best behavior and so is the other person. You're always on time. Always well dressed. You always smell good. Your hair is always perfect. You're always accommodating. You overlook and ignore your date's faults. Even if you are not a fan of the ballet, you'll go. Even if hockey is not your favorite sport, you'll watch it. I can never remember a time when my date and I went to different shows, ate at different restaurants or watched different television shows in different rooms. Yet when I got married that's often what ended up happening.

Take it from someone who has been married - dating is nothing like life during marriage. One of my clients said it best when he described dating as "the opposite sexes on their best behavior."

For those of you who are just starting to date, you may want to take this advice. Date and have fun. Meet and date many people. Don't commit yourself to one person too soon. Don't settle for the first person who comes along and tells you that you are cute. Realize that there is a whole world of interesting people out there. Enjoy!

The same rule applies for those who are separated or divorced and who begin dating again. Unfortunately, if you have been out of the dating scene for some time, you face some new problems.

One of the first problems that confronted me was just the concept of dating. After having been married and out of the "singles scene" for so many years, the thought of dating again was anything but appealing. In fact, for me it was very scary.

Then I thought, who would I date? Where would I meet someone with similar interests to mine? I couldn't see myself using dating services, logging into internet chat rooms or frequenting pubs and singles dances to meet women I had nothing in common with. A friend then suggested that I forget the traditional venues and visit places were I could meet people who had interests similar to mine. That same friend asked me what I enjoyed doing. I told him I enjoy grocery shopping. He told me to think of supermarkets as more than just places to buy groceries. So, taking his advice, the next time I went shopping I decided to lift my eyes out of the shopping cart and look around a little. Wow! All of a sudden, right before my eyes were many eligible women who also enjoyed shopping. I began to strike up conversations with them. Many women were surprised to find a man who enjoyed and actually did the grocery shopping. We talked about prices, recipes and the different places we like to shop. The supermarket turned out to be a great place to meet many eligible women.

As time passed I used that friend's suggestion more and more. I love to fly airplanes as a hobby so I looked at my flying club as more than just a place to rent an airplane. Visiting the flying club became a social event. I was surprised to discover how many female pilots and pilot trainees there were. I spoke with many of them and had wonderful conversations, not just those superficial "nice weather" or "do you come here often?" conversations that people use as a prime opening line of introduction when trying to drum up conversation with someone of the opposite sex.

Being a sports car lover and motorcyclist, I repeated the same exercise at the car and motorcycle clubs. Both proved to be successful.

Since my separation, I try to meet as many new people as possible and I am having fun making new friends.

Going Steady
(But there's a whole world out there)

After dating for a while, many of us often "pair off" and begin to get serious. We start to "go steady."

If you are old enough to have teenagers, I'll bet you can remember what your parents had to say when you started to go steady. "You are getting too serious too fast." "There are many fish in the ocean." "Don't limit yourself." If you are a teenager I am sure you hear this all the time. If you are a teenager don't take this to mean your parents don't want you to be happy. The fact is they want you to be happy. Very happy. That's why they are saying these things to you. If you don't believe me, think about this – Your parents were teenagers, once upon a time. They lived through these times and many have paid a heavy price for not heading the words of their parents. Listen to my story.

I just look back on my own situation. My ex-wife was my first "pairing off" relationship. Friends would often tell me — "you're going to marry that girl" — "you're an item." I would discount those statements and tell everyone that we were just close friends. At the time, marriage was the furthest thing from my mind. As time went on and days became months and holidays were spent with both families, our relationship could best be described as "routine." Any inkling of non-compatibility was pushed aside and ignored because the relationship was "easy" and "comfortable." There was no pressure. There was no singles scene. Friends would often ask me to join them at dances and functions to meet new people, but I would refuse because of the comfort of my steady relationship. I did not want to start over again. I did not want to meet someone new and have to start making small talk and telling my date all about my past and what my interests were.

At the time, I can honestly say that I was also a little insecure about whether a girl would find me attractive. Unlike some of my friends, I never had a sister who could at least tell me what her girl-friends thought of me. You know, if I was cute or ugly. So when my ex-wife told me that I was handsome, I couldn't believe it and fell for her.

"Pairing off" and going steady is like hearing your favorite song that you know the words to and get a good feeling when you play it. But by playing this song over and over, you do so at the expense of not giving yourself the opportunity to hear other great compositions. Looking back, I now realize, when I was in my early twenties, I was not as smart as I thought I was.

My advice to young people — give your parents an open ear. Realize they have lived the experience. What they have to say comes from years of experience and most importantly, from their love for you. I am not advocating they are always right. What I am saying is at least listen and consider what they are telling you.

For those of you who are in a steady relationship, look at your relationship objectively. Confront the relationship by asking yourself the following questions — Do you really know this person? Do you really want to live with this person the rest of your life? Is this the person you want to share your good times and bad times with? Think beyond the feelings of infatuation and ask yourself if you will still be in love with this person 20 years from now. Don't just pass over these questions lightly. We are all excited when we buy a new car. Five years later many of us are ready to trade it in. Ask yourself if you are going to feel the same about this person. Take it from a lawyer and a person who has lived through a divorce — the repercussions of "trading in" your partner are not to be taken lightly. Family law is a very serious area to be thrown into.

Getting Very Very Serious
(Just a couple of steps away)

How do you know that the person you have been going steady with is Mr. or Mrs. right?

You may be in a relationship where you have been dating for some time and find yourself being pressured by your partner or by family and friends to make a more serious commitment to the relationship. What should your next move be?

Many people advocate that living together and having intimate relations is the only way to test whether or not they are compatible for the long term. For others, myself included, the only option was marriage. From what friends and clients have told me, there does not appear to be a "right" or "wrong" answer.

Some people who have chosen to live together, before getting married, have told me they avoided a divorce by opting to live together. Living together, they say, provided them with the opportunity to come to the realization they truly were not compatible.

On the other hand, one client, who had been living with someone for many years, told me there is a downside to living together. She believes because she opted to live together, her partner became so comfortable in the "living together arrangement" he never got around to making the final commitment to marriage. She told me because they had lived together for so long they missed out on having children. She refused to have children until they were legally married.

I also have clients that are the product of "old country," arranged marriages. Many of these clients, who have been married for over 50 years, claim they are very happy and would not have done anything differently.

What should you do? There is no right or wrong answer.

If you believe that living together is the best option, is not against your moral values and the opinions you treasure, then do it. But remember, in some jurisdictions, living together may trigger legal ramifications. Speak to a family law lawyer before you enter into any cohabitation arrangement. Depending upon where you live, if you choose to live together, the act of living together itself may trigger support, property and child support obligations that you may only become aware of after it is too late. Let me give you an example. In one jurisdiction, if you cohabit with a person who has a minor child that is not biologically yours, you could be liable for paying child support to that child if the relationship does not work out. Scary!

If living together is not an option, you may wish to consider a longer engagement period to get to know your future partner and their family better.

One client told me, before he made the decision to marry his wife, he opted to take a month long "sabbatical" where he spent time by himself contemplating whether or not he could live without her. After a month, he realized marriage was the only option for him. That couple is happily married to this day.

Even if you have decided this is the right person to get very serious with, ask yourself if you are moving on to the next step in the relationship for the right reasons? Before making that final commitment, I encourage you to seriously consider some of the following questions:

Ask yourself: Is this commitment you are making just an escape route from living with your parents?

Many people I know who are married and are now separated or divorced tell me one of the biggest reasons they decided to marry was because it was a convenient way to leave home, not necessarily because they were truly in love with their partner. They told me, at the time, they thought they were in love, but really, they were in love with the thought of living independently from their parents and siblings.

Sometimes parents pressure children to grow up, get married and get on with their lives. So the kids get married. The only problem with this line of thinking is if the marriage goes bad, the kids usually end up back at their parents' house, except this time it is out of necessity, not choice.

Ask yourself: Are you thinking of marriage because it is "the thing to do?"

Looking at my own circle of friends, it seems we all got married around the same time. It might have been coincidental, but I really think peer pressure had a lot to do with it. As your friends start to get married and you attend the festivities and parties, you can't help but think "this should be happening to me too." Furthermore, if you are single and your friends are married, you tend to feel like an un-welcomed stranger when you are with them because you are not one of them — "a married couple."

Ask yourself: Is this person for real?

Is the person you are going steady with the "right" person or the person you want them to be?

If you believe you are with the "right" person, have you considered and resolved these important issues?

Banking Arrangements

Are you planning to have joint or separate bank accounts? If you are going to have a mixture of both, which bank account will your pay check go into? Are you a "what is mine is mine person?" or a "what is mine is ours person?" What about your partner? These are not trivial questions. These are questions that must be confronted by every couple. If these issues are left unresolved the result could be the demise of the relationship.

What about credit cards? Are you planning to have joint credit cards or your own separate credit cards? How are you and your partner going to deal with credit cards? Are you going to pay the balance in full at the end of the month or are you going to pay the minimum and worry about the accumulated debt at a later date? If both of you are not on the same page with respect to this issue, your relationship could be undermined.

Investing and Saving

Are you a conservative investor or one who takes chances with your money? What about your partner? What if your partner is a risk taker and loses a great deal of money in a bad investment? Would you be willing to share your savings with your partner or will you take the attitude, "you lost it, too bad?" Is one of you a saver and the other a spender? If you are a saver, ask yourself if you will resent the fact that your partner spends money on items that are not necessities? How would you feel if you have always been a saver, concerned about that potential "rainy day," only to have your partner come home with expensive new clothes for a party? On the other hand, if you are both spenders, have you thought about saving for the future?

What about a budget? What about the bills?

Do both of you believe in taking the time to make a budget or will you ignore a budget and hope to have enough money each month to cover your expenses?

What expenses can you expect to have each month? If you are renting, the first priority is the rent check. If you own, you'll have the mortgage payments, taxes, insurance, utilities (gas/oil, electricity, water, cable TV, internet provider) and repairs. What about newspaper and magazine subscriptions, gifts for family and friends, student loans, wedding bills, car payments, insurance, repairs, license and gas? Other bills that really take a chunk out of your monthly budget are food, clothing and entertainment. Who is going to take the time to pay these bills each month? Which bank account will be used to pay these bills?

When you are both earning an income and have a budget and you manage to cover the budget, the bills get paid and you both have control over this responsibility. But, have you considered what would happen if one of you loses their job or develops an illness? How will the bills be paid if that happens?

What if your partner is starting a business or is in the process of expanding a current business and you are asked to sign as guarantor? Will you agree to such an arrangement and assume the responsibility if your partner defaults?

What about "money sources?"

What if your family is willing to help you out financially and the other family is not? Will this cause resentment? Will your partner feel that they are losing their independence? Will it bother you if your

15

partner spends "your parents" money? What if your partner uses some of that money to buy gifts for their side of the family?

Have you thought about your career?

If you are just finishing high school, do you have plans for college? If you are attending college is it your desire to continue to graduate school? Marriage may have a profound impact on whether you attend college or move on to graduate school.

I have a friend who got married at a young age, started her family and never went on to college. She always wanted to be a lawyer. This lady works in a law office as a secretary and to this day regrets not having put her marriage on hold to further her education.

Are you happy in the career you are in? If not, marriage may prevent you from ever changing careers. You may never have enough money to go back to school. Furthermore, any career changes you wish to make after you are married will have to be made with your partner's consent. When you are single, relocation or career changes are viable options. Marriage throws an entirely different light on the situation. You now have a life partner to deal with.

What about personal issues?

How do you get along with your future in-laws and your partner's siblings? If you sense they are controlling, this issue will not go away and will forever haunt your relationship.

What about religion? If you are of the same religion, is one of you more devoted than the other? If this is the case, have you discussed how you will resolve such issues as attendance at your place of worship, donations, volunteering and celebration of religious festivals? If one of you is more religious, it is dangerous to assume that your partner will change. Perhaps they will change, but what if they don't? Can you accept this fact? How will you feel about attending your place of worship without your partner? From what I have heard, this issue has led to the downfall of many relationships.

What if you are of different religions? Is one of you going to convert? If you do not convert will you be accepted by your partner's family? If your partner does not convert, will your family accept him/her?

What about if you have children in a mixed faith marriage? Under what religion will they be raised? How will you feel if your parents or in-laws do not approve of the faith you follow regarding the way your children are raised? Will they attempt to influence your children to their way of thinking?

What about your friends and your partner's friends?

One of my clients told me she always made a point of treating her husband's friends like family. She knew how important those friends were to him. She never made him choose between her and them like many people she knew did. When his friends came over for sporting events she gave them their space. Her husband always thanked her for being so understanding and considerate and reciprocated by treating her friends the same way.

What about free time?

It is very important to understand that once you are married "your time" becomes "our time." Once you are married you no longer have unlimited free time. Furthermore, you have to accept the fact you may, as part of the "compromise in your marriage," go to places together that you would have shunned as a single person.

Ask yourself how you might react to spending Sunday afternoons in the art gallery or museum if you find art galleries and museums boring? On the other hand, if you dislike car racing how would you feel about attending a four-hour car race with your spouse? It is important that you and your partner discuss how you will deal with such situations. If you don't, you may find yourself wrestling to free yourself from the obligations to attend functions you dislike.

One of my clients related how she and her husband dealt with this issue. She told me, every second weekend, one of them gets to choose where and what they are going to do together.

Another client told me that he and his wife have agreed to give each other one free weekend each month to do with as they please. The other weekends they spend together.

Another client told me her marriage would not have survived had she continued to pressure her husband to do things he did not want to do. At the beginning of their marriage she attempted to "culture" her husband by taking him to the opera and the ballet. As time went on she realized he was bored and becoming bitter when asked to attend these events. She came to the conclusion that "force feeding" culture on her husband was not going to work. She now attends ballet and opera with her friends and has a happy husband.

What about raising a family?

Do both of you want children? If so, when do you want to start your family? How many children? What if you both want children, but due to medical reasons, later find that it is not possible to have children? Will you accept this fact or will you resent your partner? Is adoption a possibility? How many children can you afford? If you both work, who is going to look after them? Who will care for them when they are ill? Who will pick them up from school? Who will look after them during the summer? Have you planned for their future schooling? Will they attend private or public school?

These are all issues that should be resolved before you make the commitment to marriage.

Speaking from experience as a previously married man and as a lawyer who meets with many people, if you and your partner do not confront these issues, you are both in for a rude awakening. These issues, if left unresolved, do not go away.

The Engagement
(Almost there — watch out for the warning signs)

You have come to that point in your relationship where you have decided this is the right person and it is time to settle down — so you pop the question or accept the proposal.

Congratulations are in order. It is party time. Everyone is excited and all your friends and family make a big fuss about the future couple. Not only is everyone excited, but so are you. You get caught up in the moment. Your future is full of hope and promise. You are the center of attention. The engagement period is full of festivities and happiness but, more importantly, it is a time that should be used to reflect upon yourself and your future partner as a couple. Engagement is the final step before you are legally married. It is the last opportunity to put an end to the relationship free of legal ramifications. Therefore you better be sure this is the person you want to spend the rest of your life with. It is during this time that you should

step back and take another objective look at your relationship without being blinded by romance and passion. Don't assume marriage will fix any traits in your future partner that you don't care for now. Many couples get married under the false assumption that they will be able to "change" their partner. Speaking from experience and from what I have heard, it is unlikely this will happen. Of course, I make this statement with one proviso in mind — some people do change. Still, I will never forget the words of my grandfather who had this to say about change — "it is impossible to change the spots on a leopard."

The Warning Signs: Questions to Ask

Every day of the engagement period should be spent carefully evaluating whether or not you are making the right choice. Yes, everyday!

Does your future partner's habit of always being late bother you? If it bothers you now, understand it will probably not go away after you are married. The fact is, it will most likely lead to arguments and resentment.

Does the fact your future partner spends Friday nights out with the boys upset you? Will it bother you if he continues this practice after you are married? If it does, will you quarrel about it?

Does your fiancé constantly call you and keep track of where you are? If it bothers you now, remember this practice will likely continue after you are married.

Ask yourself if the attraction to your future spouse is only physical? If this is the case, consider whether you should be committing yourself to this person when there are thousands of other physically attractive people out there.

Maybe you are getting married for the wrong reason. Have you asked yourself if you are marrying this person because they or their family have money? If this is the case, be aware of what many clients have told me about "marrying money." They noted after they were married they had to work for every cent they thought they were going to get.

Let's take this one step further. If you are convinced this person is physically and emotionally attractive to you, ask yourself if you truly want to be with this person if that person gets sick or loses his or her job. More importantly, if you have an independent personality and value your free time, are you ready to go from being a "sole proprietor" to a "50/50 partnership?"

I personally know of couples who broke off their wedding plans during the engagement because things just weren't right.

One of my divorced clients told me he wishes he had spent some time looking objectively at his relationship during the engagement. He told me he believed that "things would get better" after he got married. He did not want to break up during the engagement period and embarrass himself and his family.

Another client told me she and her fiancé broke off the engagement twice yet still ended up getting married, had four children and are now divorced. She told me she broke off her engagement twice because of arguments over money. Her fiancé promised her he would change his spending habits and become more of a saver after they got married. She told me she believed him, then she married him and he never changed. She told me she ignored the warning signs.

Speaking of warning signs, now would be a good time to look at some warning signs clients and friends have passed on to me. Here are a few interesting ones.

One of my clients relayed an interesting story that should have been a signal to her. At her engagement party, her then fiancé drank to excess and embarrassed her with his behavior. He mocked her and made jokes about marriage. She told me in her heart she felt there was something wrong with the relationship, but dismissed his behavior as just a young man having a good time. She is now divorced and noted that throughout their marriage he got drunk at parties and routinely came home and hit the bottle.

Another client noted his fiancé had a personality transformation, as he says, "once she felt she had me." The sweet, accommodating, wonderful young lady, he once knew became demanding, selfish and moody. He told me he had absolutely no say in the wedding plans. She and her mother wanted the wedding done their way and expected his parents to simply sign the check for half of the expenses. He is now in the process of divorcing her. Her behavior, he dismissed, at the time, as wedding stress, was actually the real her. He told me she controlled the kind of house they bought, how it was furnished, when they moved into the house, and so on.

Another person told me the story of how naïve she was for believing in her husband who did nothing but dream of success. She met him when he was in his early 20s. He always claimed they would have nothing to worry about in the future because he was going to, as he put it, "make it big." During their engagement he could not hold a job, but told her never to worry because he claimed he was a "millionaire in training." For 15 years, she accepted his excuses and optimistic attitude and believed in him. As it turned out, the only money he could make was the money he asked her to ask her parents for. They are now divorced.

A friend, let's call her Sue, did not discover that her fiancé was gay until after they were married. She ignored the warning signs during the engagement period. Her fiancé had little or no interest in being intimate with her. He told her he wanted to wait until after they were married before engaging in sexual relations. Until the wedding, he acted like a brother and a good friend. They are now divorced.

Keep a sharp eye out for evidence of a temper. I have heard many stories of people who are supposedly on their best behavior during the engagement period, but "lose it" every once in a while, often over trivial matters. It may be over a discussion about the flower arrangements at the wedding, what a family member may have said, a gift you have to buy for someone or what television show you will watch. Sometimes it is sulking. Sometimes it is the silent treatment or other times it may be a slamming car door or a bang of the telephone receiver. Obviously everyone is entitled to have a bad day once in a while but if the behavior persists, it may be an indicator of things to come. Such behavior often escalates and can destroy a marriage because it may become unbearable to live with.

One of my clients told me about a warning sign that I have heard from others as well. She told me, during her engagement period, her ex-spouse kept comparing her to an old girlfriend. At the time she thought nothing of it and dismissed this infatuation with his old flame as unimportant believing he would forget about her after their marriage. He never did. After they separated he started dating his old flame again. She told me she realizes now they were never meant to be.

Another client told me she was a neat freak and her fiancé was the complete opposite. This opposite behavior was never an issue during their engagement. It only hit home when they got married and began to live together. She told me after five years of picking up his clothes, organizing his drawers and cleaning up after him she just couldn't take it anymore. They are now divorced. She told me she should have paid more attention to the fact they were so opposite on this issue. In some cases opposites don't attract!

The last warning sign to leave you with is a good one. This warning sign deals with your potential new family. How do you and your future in-laws and family get along? Are they controlling? Do they make you feel at home when you visit or do they make you feel like leaving as soon as you get there?

One of my clients told me that she never felt comfortable at her future in-laws. Her in-laws never seemed to warm up to her or accept her as a member of the family during the engagement period. She told me at her engagement party she was made to feel more like an acquaintance than a member of the family. This continued after the marriage despite the welcoming words expressed at the wedding. She believes her husband decided to separate from her because of his family.

All this is not to frighten or dissuade you from marriage. I have raised these points so you can give them consideration. Too many people, in my opinion, end up getting married without ever having considered these warning signs and are later sorry for not having given them a second thought.

During the engagement period, it is almost impossible to imagine the person you are going to marry could ever end up becoming your worse nightmare. Just ask anyone who has lived through a bad divorce. It is a fact of life that many marriages just don't work out. It is equally important to realize that if you take a little time before you get married to become aware of how marriage and the law works, you may be able to minimize the damage and know what you are in for, especially if things don't work out.

Let's look at some of those legal realities.

The Legal Realities of Marriage

Once you are married, you and your spouse acquire a special status under the law. Marriage is a legal partnership and with it come new rights and obligations involving issues such as property, spousal and/or child support, and estate matters.

I encourage you to become informed and protect yourself with respect to the law as it applies to marriage. Take advantage of all the legal safeguards offered by the laws in your jurisdiction if you are getting married. Marriage is not only about love! It is also a legal relationship.

The Pre-Nuptial Agreement

Speak to a family law lawyer about the value of a pre-nuptial agreement and how it can protect you.

A pre-nuptial agreement is an agreement between you and your future spouse that establishes rights and obligations involving issues such as property, support and children during the marriage. In addition, a pre-nuptial agreement often addresses the rights and obligations of the parties in the event the marriage breaks down. You may think this is not a topic to be discussed at the same time you are choosing the menu for the wedding. In fact, you may believe raising this issue may dampen or even cancel the wedding plans. In some cases, it does. A pre-nuptial agreement brings to light the legal realities of marriage and highlights all the issues that will have to be addressed in the event of a marital breakdown.

A pre-nuptial agreement will involve negotiation. It will force you and your partner to disclose everything you own and are bringing into the marriage. If you opt for a pre-nup, you and your partner will likely have your own lawyers. This is the ideal situation to ensure you both get independent legal advice. You may find the process tedious, time consuming, unnerving and expensive. In the end you and your partner may decide to abandon the idea of an agreement altogether. On the other hand, both of you may conclude the time and money spent on this exercise has brought you closer together and the contract itself provides peace of mind so that you both know where you stand in the relationship.

Depending upon where you live, it may be possible to sign a marriage agreement after you are married. The problem with waiting until after you are married to sign a marriage agreement is both you and your spouse may not be as motivated to enter into such an agreement at that time. It is important to remember after you are married, even if you are motivated to sign one of these agreements, your spouse may not be. Once married, it may be too late. You cannot force your unwilling spouse to sign a marriage agreement.

In addition to agreements, there are other legal issues that you should consider prior to getting married. Here are a few that you may not have thought of.

The Home

Did you know that, depending upon where you live, the home you live in after you are married takes on a special legal status? In many jurisdictions, the home is treated differently than any other asset. In those jurisdictions, once you are married and live in that house as a couple, you both automatically acquire a legal interest in that home regardless of who owns the house. This means if you separate, even if  legal title to the house is in your name, your spouse may be entitled to a 50% interest in that home just because you are married.

Items owned prior to marriage and gifts received after marriage

It is important to keep a record of all the things you own before marriage.

In many jurisdictions, property acquired before marriage (except the family home) may not have to be shared with a spouse in the event of separation. When a couple separate, each is required to complete a financial statement where they record what they own at the date of separation and what they owned on the date of marriage. The court then subtracts what they owned on the date of marriage from what they owned on the date of separation. Without a record of what you owned on the date of marriage, you will be unable to deduct what you brought into the marriage from what you owned on the date of separation. One of my clients learned this lesson the hard way. He had been married for over twelve years. Never giving divorce a second thought, he discarded all his bank records when he got married. His ex kept all her records. This poor fellow had over $50,000 dollars in his own bank account when he got married but without his bank records was unable to deduct this money from what he owned on the date of separation. His bank routinely destroyed all records every 7 years.

It is equally important to document all of your personal effects that you bring into the marriage. In so doing there is no question as to what belongs to you and what belongs to your spouse.

In short, before you get married, take the time to record all of the things you own on the date of marriage, which includes bank balances, property and a list of personal effects and be sure to put that record in a safe place.

It is also important to keep a record of all personal gifts received after marriage. In many jurisdictions, gifts acquired during the marriage may be considered excluded property if there is a marriage breakdown.

What about your will?

Are you aware that, in many jurisdictions, marriage cancels a will made before the date of marriage? Furthermore, depending upon where you live, if you pass away without a will, the law sets out what your spouse is entitled to inherit from your estate. Many people are surprised to learn, depending on where you live, your spouse may not necessarily inherit your entire estate should you be the first to die. Furthermore, if you and your spouse die together in a common accident and you have no children or they die at the same time as you do and if your spouse dies after you, your spouse's family could end up inheriting your entire estate to the  exclusion of your own family. How many of you care for your in-laws that much?

Many of my clients are surprised to learn the moment they are married, they no longer have the right to do as they please with the things they own when they die. In fact, in most jurisdictions, individuals are prohibited from cutting out their spouses in their will. In most jurisdictions, a spouse does not have to accept what is left to them in their spouse's will. In such jurisdictions, a spouse has what is known as "the right to make an election." This means that a spouse has a choice to take either what is left to them in the deceased spouse's will or take what he or she is entitled to under the law. Speak to your family law lawyer about using a pre-nuptial or marriage agreement to "free your hand" when it comes to making your will.

What about giving gifts to children who are getting married?

If you intend to give a gift to your child who is planning to marry, consult a family law lawyer BEFORE you make this gift. The lawyer will advise when you should make this gift (before marriage or after marriage) and will prepare any legal documentation required to ensure that the gift always remains with your child in the event of a marital breakdown. In  many jurisdictions, a gift given after marriage does not enter the financial equation in the event of a marital breakdown provided the gift is properly recorded and is not used in any way towards the purchase or improvement of the family home. Paying off the mortgage on the matrimonial home would, in many jurisdictions, not be excluded from net family property.

Be careful. Get some advice from a family law lawyer before you make any substantial gifts to your child and their spouse.

I know of many individuals who want to purchase a home for their children or give them a substantial down payment. Stop! Speak to a lawyer before you do. Your lawyer may advise you to set the transaction up as a loan or provide you with an interest in the property just in case the marriage does not work out.

It is equally important to inquire if the laws where you live allow you to include special wording in your will to protect your married child's inheritance. Depending upon where you live, if a parent passes away and leaves a will without this special wording, a daughter-in-law or son-in-law could end up benefiting from what you leave your child in your will.

This is by no means an exhaustive list of issues that you should consider. It is for this reason that I urge you to consult with a lawyer before you get married. Not only should you make the time to see a lawyer, but make the visit alone, without your fiancé. If you are a parent, encourage your child to visit with a family law lawyer before they are married, even if you have to pay for the consultation. Trust me, if your child does not take this step and the marriage does not work out, your child will, most likely, end up on your doorstep asking why you never warned them.

The Marriage
(Making it work)

Congratulations. You are now legally married and are legal partners in the eyes of the law.

I can recall when my ex-wife and I returned home from our honeymoon. It was only at that time the reality of marriage began to sink in. We were a Mr. and Mrs.. In fact, I will never forget the first envelope addressed to us as a couple. I must say when I saw that envelope it excited me — after all, I had just entered a new phase of my life.

Once we were married, it seemed that every step we made as a couple was like a baby learning to walk. Each step was new and uneasy, and both of us were unsure of where it would lead us.

Since we opted not to live together prior to marriage, many issues had to be worked out for the first time. For example, some of the issues that confronted us were: Which side of the bed we slept on. The number of pillows on the bed. The number of comforters on the bed. The time we went to bed and the time we woke up. Whether we would wake up to an alarm or music. The temperature we would set the thermostat to. What closet each of us took and how much closet space we each would take. Whether there would be a television in our bedroom or not. Whether we would watch television or read a book before going to bed. Who would take out the trash. Who would do the grocery shopping. Who would do the paperwork and pay the bills. What colors the rooms would be painted. What style of furniture to buy. And so on — I am sure every married couple can relate and even add a few other issues to this list. This is not to say these issues created animosity. They were just issues that had to be discussed and resolved.

Anyone who is or has been married will tell you marriage is a partnership. Once you are married you are no longer on your own and must recognize that you are living with another person and that each person has their own unique personality. One of my clients noted that if a marriage is going to succeed, it requires each partner to give and take and, most importantly, to love and respect each other. Unfortunately, my marriage did not work out. But many marriages do. I have always wondered what the secret is to a good marriage. As a lawyer, I see many married couples, some of whom have been married for a long time. I always take a few moments to ask them about the secret to the longevity of their marriage.

Here is what I have heard:

Take An Interest

Take an interest in what interests your spouse. One client noted how much his wife liked attending live theater so whenever a good show came to town he made sure that he would purchase tickets and treat his wife to an evening out.

Be Reasonable In Your Expectations

As one client told me, "you never marry a perfect human being." She went on to say, "everyone has their faults — recognize that you are not perfect and overlook your spouse's faults, otherwise your marriage is doomed to fail." She noted there were many times she felt like walking out of her marriage, but stopped short of doing so, realizing she was not always the easiest person to live with. One couple told me the key to their successful marriage was due to the fact they shared all their responsibilities equally and if one ended up pulling more weight than the other, they never forgot to say "thank you."

Never Stay Angry

Every couple has disagreements, but the key to a happy marriage, I am told, is to forgive and forget. One client, who had a very happy marriage, left me with this thought — "remember the good times for a long time and remember the bad times for a short time."

Provide Breathing Space

One couple told me they live by the motto, "if you love something, let it be free." This couple, who have been married for a long time, realized early in their marriage they did not necessarily have to do everything together. In fact, they both recognized that a healthy balance of time together and time away from each other strengthened their relationship.

Keep Differences Private

Never embarrass your partner — One couple noted they never argued or criticized the other in public. They adopted this policy after witnessing one of their friends mocking her spouse at a company party and thinking how terrible the other must have felt. This policy has proved to solidify their relationship. Many couples have told me they make it a point of never discussing a private issue in public.

Don't Live In The Past

History is for historians not for married couples — One couple noted they never raised old battles and old wounds but always looked towards bettering their relationship. This they maintain is the key to their successful marriage.

Focus on Keeping Each Other Happy

Love is deeper than a hug or a kiss. I just look at my parents. I cannot remember the last time I saw them kiss each other, yet they both routinely look at each other with love in their hearts. They don't show their affections outwardly, but both express their love for each other in what they do and what they say. Their relationship grows every day because they spend their time focused on making each other happy and not thinking about themselves.

Be a Good Listener

Be an "active listener" — One couple told me they always listened to what the other had to say. They regularly sit together during dinner to discuss what happened to each other that day. They attribute their long, happy marriage to this practice.

Recognize Your Spouse's Accomplishments

Recognize the accomplishments of each other — One client told me she will never forget her husband telling her how proud he was that she won the best quilting award at a local fair. She was a stay at home mom and this compliment meant a great deal to her. She told me that she has told her own married children of the importance of complimenting their spouses.

Be a Team Player

Raising children is a "team" effort. Many of my clients, who have children, noted the importance of a team approach when it came to raising their children. These couples stuck together  when it came to discipline and shared all parenting responsibilities such as making lunches, carpooling and attending parent's night.

Take Time For Each Other

Make a date with each other — One close friend of mine told me she and her husband made a point of setting aside a few hours each week from their busy schedule to spend some quiet time together away from the house. She told me an evening out did not have to be spent at an expensive restaurant or enjoying an expensive night on the town. A coffee together at a local coffee shop was all they needed. One client noted she and her husband made a point of having breakfast together at least a few times a week. They made a habit of reading the morning newspaper together and talked about local and world events. She said this exercise brought them closer together because it gave them things to talk about. She said they do not always agree on every issue but their discussions serve to solidify their relationship.

Focus on The Future Together

Build a life together — I first heard this from a couple who have been married for over 60 years. I have heard similar statements from other happily married couples. The couple I am referring to were married just prior to World War II. He went overseas and his new bride kept the home fires burning. They both vowed when the war was over, they would build a life together. After the war, he started a small tailor shop and his wife worked alongside him. They saved their money, bought a small home, started a family, worked long hours and noted that it was not her life or his life but life together that made for a successful marriage.

Never Take Your Marriage For Granted

Nurture your marriage — One couple married for a very long time told me they remained married because they never took each other or their marriage for granted. They made each other and their relationship a priority in their lives.

These are a few insights that I have learned about. It is my hope that you can benefit from them.

Other Considerations You May Face
as a Married Couple

Let's look at some other considerations you may face as a married couple.

If you are purchasing a house or condominium, speak to your lawyer and discuss how the title to the property should be registered. You must decide if it should be registered as joint owners with right of survivorship or as tenants-in-common. Joint ownership with right of survivorship means that if one of the spouses dies, the other spouse automatically becomes the legal owner of the property. On the other hand, if the property is registered as tenants-in-common, that means one spouse owns a share of the property. When a property is registered as tenants in common, if one of the spouses dies, the other spouse does not automatically become the legal owner of the entire property, as is the case, if it is registered as joint owners. If you opt to register the property as tenants-in-common, your will determines who gets your share of the property upon your death and your spouse's will determines who gets their share of the property.

As soon as you get married you should consider preparing powers of attorney and a will.

A power of attorney is a document you need to have in place so someone can make financial decisions for you in the event you are unable to make these decisions for yourself due to an accident or illness. Without this legal document known as a durable or continuing power of attorney, the government could end up making financial decisions for you to the exclusion of your spouse and family. Your assets may be frozen or in some cases, depending upon where you live, the government could end up becoming the manager of your financial affairs, which includes all banking and investment decisions. Without this document in place, your spouse may be forced to go to court in order to obtain the power to act on your behalf. In a durable or continuing power of attorney, you can appoint your spouse, trusted love one or friend to act on your behalf with respect to your financial affairs in the event you become incapable. It is important to note if you become incapable it is too late to take advantage of this protection.

Depending upon where you live, you may be permitted to make another type of power of attorney known as a durable power of attorney for health care. This document, also known as a health and personal care proxy, enables you to legally appoint your spouse, trusted loved one or friend to become your health care agent. Your health care agent will have the legal authority to deal with doctors, hospitals or nursing homes on your behalf. In many jurisdictions you may also be allowed to make what is commonly known as a "living will." A "living will" sets out your wishes as they relate to a situation where you are so ill that there is no hope for recovery. You may set out, for example, that you do not want to be kept alive by artificial means or life support.

What if you die? When you die, your powers of attorney die with you and then your will takes effect. Both you and your spouse need your own wills.

As a lawyer, I find many couples are under the assumption they do not need a will. If you die without a will, the law writes one for you and sets out who inherits from your estate. Don't assume your spouse will automatically inherit everything you own if you die without a will. In many jurisdictions, a surviving spouse is only entitled to a portion of your estate. Furthermore, depending upon where you live, if you have minor children and you pass away without a will, your children could become wards of the state. In many jurisdictions, if you do not have a will and you leave minor children, all your assets, including family heirlooms have to be sold. The money from the sale of those assets is then managed by a government agency for the children until they reach the age of majority. Meanwhile, that same government agency takes a chunk of your children's money as a fee for this service.

Don't assume that you are saving money by not writing a will. In most cases if you pass away without a will, attorney fees will most likely be double or triple what they would have been had you taken the time to write a will. That's why it is important to make a will.

When you prepare a will, you are going to appoint an executor who will look after your estate. Of course, the logical choice is your spouse.

Your will sets out who is going to benefit from your estate. In your will, you can also appoint a legal guardian for your minor children in the event both you and your spouse pass away in a common accident.

As a wills lawyer, I can assure you that every person, no matter if they are young or old, land owners or tenants, needs a will. To pass away without a will is one of the most horrible "legacies" you can leave behind for your loved ones.

Let's now look at a few other issues that you will face as a married couple.

One issue that cannot be ignored is the issue of money. Will you live for the day, save for a rainy day or fall somewhere in between? Whatever path you choose must be a joint decision if your marriage is going to last. Many couples have told me their marriage failed because they were in two different worlds when it came to the issue of money.

Equally important is the decision you both make about where you are going to live.

If you have decided home ownership is the way to go, the type of house and cost of that home will be factors that confront you. Are you both willing to purchase a modest sized home that is affordable with little or no mortgage or will you risk being "house poor" by opting for a home with a large mortgage that you can barely afford? One couple told me, to this day, they regret having bought a big house with a small down payment because their mortgage payment ate up a big chunk of their monthly budget leaving them with little extra money for other things.

Then there is the issue of children. Do you both want children? If you do, are you going to start your family right away or are you going to wait? There is no right answer

to this question. Of course, there are many factors that affect your decision. Money, your career, and issues such as who will look after the child are all factors that come into play when and if you begin a family.

There will be times during your marriage when you may feel you are up against issues that seem anything but resolvable. How do couples resolve major differences? Some opt to ignore them in the hope they will go away. Others will "bend the branch" as far as it will go until one gives in. Many take the team approach, compromise and work out a solution that works for both parties. Some couples seek outside help like mediation or marriage counseling. Other couples make the dangerous assumption the answer to a troubled marriage is starting a family and hoping that a child will bring the couple closer together. In some cases, a child may help the couple work out their differences. However, from those couples I have spoken to who that have opted for children in the hope of a better marriage, it has proven to be a mistake. Children are a huge responsibility and can strain even the most solid relationships. When couples break up after having had children, there is usually a custody battle over those children and there are usually everlasting emotional scars left upon those children.

What if the Marriage Doesn't Work Out?
(It takes two people to marry but only one to divide the family in half)

Unlike previous generations where the vast majority of couples worked out their marital problems and stuck it out through thick and thin, many married couples today choose to separate rather than work on saving their marriage.

Contrary to what many people believe, separation is not an "easy out" to marital problems. Separation has devastating consequences (emotional and financial) not only to the couple and their children but also to the couple's family and friends.

Let's face it, some marriages are so bad separation is the only solution. Nevertheless, take it from me, a lawyer and a person who has lived through a separation firsthand, unless your situation is unbearable, separation should only be used as a last resort where there is no other viable option. Anyone who wants to save their marriage should never use separation or even the threat of separation as a way of resolving marital problems. The threat of separation or even a trial separation can leave deep wounds that take a great deal of time to heal, if they ever heal at all.

One of the most important lessons I learned during my separation is it takes two consenting people to marry, but it only takes one of those people to put an end to the marriage.

Every couple has their share of disagreements and, often, time solves their differences. On the other hand, many couples reach a point in their marriage where they know in their hearts their marriage is on the "slippery slope" of decline and is headed for separation. In some marriages, both partners may not necessarily be unhappy. In these situations, separation often comes as a surprise to the partner who is oblivious to the other partner's unhappiness. As one of my clients told me, he was "blind sided" when he received a letter from his wife's attorney asking for a separation. Many of my clients who have asked me to draft a new will for them after separation have told me their separation came as a surprise. Many told me, upon reflection, there were indicators that should have alerted them to the fact their spouse may have had unilateral ideas of separating. Let's look at some of the indicators…

• Losing Touch

A number of clients noted that communication suddenly came to an end in their relationship. They noted they could be in the same room and not speak. They would go out for dinner and not have anything to say to one another.

Their spouse lost interest in the day-to-day running of the home and issues related to the children. Another client told me the "indicator light" should have gone on when all she got were short and sarcastic replies to questions posed to her husband.

• A Sudden Interest In High Tech

The internet is a great source of information, but it would appear that it also has a dark side when it comes to some marriages. Many clients told me they lost their spouses to cyber dating and cyber sex sites. They told me they were unaware of what their spouses were doing on the computer until it was too late. Others told me the cell phone played a role in the destruction of their marriage. One client told me his wife was insistent on getting a cell phone so she could get in touch with the baby sitter in the event of an emergency. As it turned out her phone became a direct link to her new boyfriend.

• The Pre-occupied Mind

Does your spouse appear to be in another world? Has there been a drastic change in his/her personality? Are they less interested in their work or business? Have others noted that your spouse is acting "differently?" These are just a few of the questions that many of my separated clients have told me they should have been asking themselves before they learned that their marriage was ending.

• A Sudden Interest In Looking Fashionable

"My husband of 25 years who never took an interest in how he looked suddenly was into designer label clothes and shopping," claimed one of my clients whose husband eventually left her for another woman. She was not alone. Another client told me her husband suddenly became interested in a hair transplant. He eventually left the relationship. Another client told me his wife insisted on withdrawing a large amount of money out of their nest egg to pay for her liposuction and breast augmentation surgery. Nine months later he received a letter from her lawyer asking for a separation.

• Loss of Interest In Being Intimate

A relationship that was at one time intimate, suddenly became bitterly cold, noted one of my clients who recently became separated. She told me her husband developed the habit of working late every night, went into the office on weekends, was always tired and told her he was burnt out. He claimed he had to work long hours for the sake of his job and to support the family. She believed him because she loved and trusted him. She was in tears as she told me that she learned her husband had been deceiving her. He was really having intimate relations with someone else.

What Separation Feels Like

I will never forget the day my ex-wife said to me that she could not live with me any more and was going to visit with a lawyer to begin separation proceedings. I was ambushed and felt like a deer frozen in headlights. Like most marriages, our marriage had been going through some rough times, but I never expected that she would ever take this step. Separation prior to this point was not a subject we discussed. She never threatened separation unless I changed, nor did I. Separation came out of the blue. I must admit I really never saw any of the indicators. I always thought we could work things out. Maybe I was naïve, but I never saw my marriage as something that would end. I always believed in the vow "till death do us part." I know that I was not the most perfect person to live with, but who is perfect?

Being separated and living under the same roof is very traumatic. My clothes were still in our closet. All my personal belongings and my life were in that house. Many thoughts crossed my mind. How would I react to my wife when I passed her in the hallway? Would I eat dinner with her and the kids or by myself after they had left the room? Would I watch television as a family or by myself? Would I leave the house and risk that she could change the locks and throw my clothes and personal effects out the door? Let me tell you from first hand experience, it is a terribly sickening predicament.

The next thing that went through my mind was the children. Would we tell the children together or tell them as individuals that their mommy and daddy were splitting? How would the kids react? How was I going to feel about not being with my children every day and not being able to sit down with them at dinner every night to discuss how their day went? How would I react to the possibility of another man moving into my house and acting as a stepfather to my children? I thought of my parents who were smiling with pride at my wedding. What were they going to say? How would they react to the possibility of seeing their grandchildren only a few times a month or at all? How was I going to react when I saw my in-laws? Would they place all the blame on me for their daughter's unhappy marriage? What about my brothers-in-law and sisters-in-law who spent holidays and special occasions with us? Would they now look at me as a stranger and outsider? What about my friends? They always thought we were so happy. How would they react? Will I ever meet anyone else?

I can honestly say, looking back on that time, I was in shock. As I sat in my family room I started to see everything as hers and mine and not ours anymore. I questioned, "would that be my sofa or hers?" "Would that be my stereo or hers?"

At the same time I couldn't help but wonder what she was feeling. What prompted her to make the decision that day? Was it something I said? Something I did? Did she have someone else? Did she understand what separation really meant? Did a visit with a lawyer prompt her to make the decision to separate or was it a friend or family member or a combination? Did she understand the ramifications of the family being broken up forever? Did she think about the fact there would be no more family dinners together? No more family vacations. Did she consider the children's lives would be divided in two — part of the time with mommy and part of the time with daddy? Did she consider the financial cost of the separation to not only me, but to her? Did she think about the financial consequences for our children's future? Did she realize that a large chunk of what we had saved could, in the end, be eaten up in lawyers' fees? Did she realize that by splitting the home she in fact doubled our expenses so that our children would never have financially what they would have otherwise?

Did she think about the possible impact of introducing another man into my children's lives? Did she think about the responsibility around the care of the children and the care of the house without me around? Did she have any concern about me, the man she had lived with for 12 years and the father of her children? Did she have any sadness or remorse or was it a happy moment for her? Did she replay the wedding day, the purchase of our first home and recall the joy experienced when our children were born like I did? Did she remember the special moments such as when I held her hand during childbirth or did she forget the good times and replace them with bad thoughts?

This is what I was thinking, but let me tell you what in fact happened.

After my wife advised me that she wanted a separation, I was told all future communication would strictly be between our lawyers. There was never a hint of compromise and there was no indication my wife wanted to separate amicably. From a lawyer's perspective, once one of the parties sets the "my way or no way" hard bargaining tone, the other party has no choice but to react in a similar manner or find themselves on the losing end of the situation. This is what happened to me.

Once I realized my wife was not open to reconciliation, I made attempts to solve many of the issues in a compromising fashion. Once I realized this approach would not work, I had no choice but to retain a lawyer who had a reputation for being just as strong as her lawyer. Every time her lawyer sent me a letter, my lawyer did the same. Some days I would get two, sometimes three letters, and it got to the point where I did not even consider I had to pay my lawyer for every letter she wrote. I just wanted my lawyer to reply equally as tough to the letters I received from her lawyer. Let me tell you what you never see in a movie or television show about marriage break-downs. The process does not end in one episode. It can go on and on. It can consume you from the minute you wake up and continue even into your dreams while you sleep, if you are able to sleep. You think about it when you are driving or talking to people. It never lets up. You begin to befriend people who are separated. You listen to their stories and compare them to your own. You dread the phone ringing, looking at your message box, passing by the fax machine and looking at your emails. The process takes over your life. Rather than thinking about my children, my parents, my friends and myself, I was thinking about how I would react to the next letter, what the next letter would contain and what my "strategy" would be. Your whole life is put on hold to accomplish one thing and that is, never to cave in and show weakness but to win at all costs. There are times when you get nostalgic when you look at a photograph or a home movie and you cannot believe what is happening. It is like a night-mare, "something that only others go through, not me." You keep saying to yourself that this will eventually go away because she must feel the same way.

Oh, those letters. As I write this my stomach still churns from the pain they caused. What was the subject matter of those letters? They wanted a valuation of everything I owned on the date of marriage (that's why I told you about the importance of keeping records of what you own before you are married and gifts received during the marriage). Letters asking for a valuation of everything I owned on the date of separation (my pension, my business, my vehicles, my law practice, etc). It is an endless spending spree. I was not qualified to value my pension, my vehicle, my business and my law practice. Thousands of dollars were spent on accountants and valuators. It did not end there because my valuators and accountants were challenged by hers. And on and on it went to the point that we began arguing about the value of china figurines. It becomes a battle where everything is fair game. All of a sudden my whole life was under a microscope being reviewed by her lawyer, a stranger, a person I had never met. That person now knew every intimate detail about my life. What I had. What I earned. How often we had intimate relations. What we thought of each other's parents and family members, our career aspirations, and so on. To make matters even worse, once our case was assigned a court file number, most of this information became a matter of public record and anyone had the right to examine it. Now anyone could find out how much money my wife and I earned, how much we had in savings, the size of our mortgage, the value of our pensions, the amount of life insurance we had and more. Think about that the next time you tell your spouse something that you never want repeated.

The letters were not just restricted to assets. They concerned matters such as when I would see my children, child support and what topics I could and could not discuss with my children. In an attempt to strengthen her case, there were letters that described my behavior towards her and towards the children from her point of view. It is interesting to note that after being married for over 12 years and being in a marriage where we both shared the responsibilities of shopping, cleaning, cooking, caring for the children and earning a living, not one letter had one positive thing to say about me. It was as if my wife had married a monster. It really hurt and at times I began to doubt myself and believe that the accusations were true. As a means of gaining emotional support and to take away some of the pain, I began to share the contents of the letters with friends and family. Sometimes they reacted positively but other times I got the feeling they began to believe them too.

Then another letter arrives, and it goes on and on.

Many of you may be under the impression you can choose to ignore these letters. You cannot. If you opt to ignore the letters it could have a very detrimental affect on your case if it goes to court. A judge may take the position you are uncooperative and want to prolong the matter. This meant after I received a letter, it was not uncommon for me to contact my lawyer immediately and spend time and money plotting how to respond.

As the letters pile up you begin to develop a dislike for the other lawyer. Then you remind yourself, he's just the mouthpiece. It was my wife who was directing him and approving all these letters. Then I began to ask myself, who is this person (my wife)? What happened to her? What happened to us? Is this really the mother of my children? She was such a wonderful person. How did love turn into hate? Then reality kicks in and you keep instructing your lawyer to do whatever it takes to get this person out of your life. The problem is if there are children, that spouse is never out of your life.

So far I have described my separation which, unfortunately, was not amicable. My ex-wife and I were unable to come to terms on the major issues with respect to our separation and every step we took on major issues involved our lawyers. That is not to say all couples who are separating must follow this route which is referred to as a contested separation and divorce. A contested separation and divorce does not mean that one of the parties is trying to prevent the divorce. It means that the couple cannot agree on matters related to the children and child support (if applicable), spousal support (if applicable) and the division of property. In a contested matter, if the couple cannot reach an agreement with the help of their lawyers, then a judge will decide for them.

In my case, my wife and I were negotiating right up to the last minute prior to the trial. It is important to realize that in many jurisdictions, many couples are motivated to settle before going to trial because of a legal rule dealing with lawyer fees and court costs. The rule has been established to encourage couples to settle on their own without having to have a judge settle the matter for them. The rule motivates a party to settle because, to put it simply, it penalizes a party who rejects a reasonable offer.

Nevertheless there are still some headstrong people who have so much bottled up anger and animosity towards their spouse that they reject even a reasonable offer just so they can have their day in court. Unfortunately many learn the impact of the rule the hard way when they end up getting less than what they were offered and are forced to pick up the tab of their lawyer, their spouse's lawyer and additional court costs awarded by the judge.

You may think you have the best case in the world but it is important to remember that judges are people and the judge may not believe your case is as strong as you think it is. If you or your spouse or both of you choose to go the contested route and are determined to win at all costs, be prepared for a large legal bill at the end of the day. When it comes to legal costs on matters that you should be able to settle, the sky is the limit if you opt for the contested route.

As a lawyer, I should not have been surprised by what I experienced. It is, after all, a lawyer's job to get the best possible deal for their client. The problem with setting an adversarial tone with your spouse is that, in most cases, it jeopardizes the slightest hope that you will ever be civil to one another again.

So what is the alternative to a contested separation and divorce? An uncontested separation and divorce. An uncontested matter means the couple settle upon matters related to the children and child support (if applicable), spousal support (if applicable) and the division of property by themselves, often with the guidance of their attorneys or a mediator. I only wish my wife and I could have traveled down this road. An uncontested matter simplifies the process and minimizes legal fees. Most importantly, it preserves whatever is left of any relationship between the parties. This is especially important where there are children involved. It also leaves the parties with a feeling of satisfaction because they both reach a satisfactory deal as opposed to one winning and one losing.

Just because you are separated does not mean that you are divorced. Just because you are separated does not mean that you have to get divorced either. In fact, some couples do reconcile after having been separated. Others choose to remain separated their entire lives and never legally terminate their marriage. But then again, in many cases, separation is just a step on the way to divorce.

What is Divorce?
(Now you are a former spouse)

By definition, divorce is the legal end of the marriage. Now s/he is your former spouse.

Being divorced does not necessarily mean all ties from your former marriage are cut. You may have spousal support obligations. If there are children, you may have child support obligations and be forced to interact with your former spouse regarding matters such as visitation, custody and special events.

Many clients told me when they chose to divorce they were under the assumption the divorce would mark the end of the relationship and provide them with an opportunity to make a new start in their lives. Unfortunately, many learned divorce does not end the relationship, it just re-defines it. Let me explain.

I will never forget the client who visited me to draft her will. She had been married for 12 years and is now divorced. She was awarded spousal support and child support indexed to her ex-husband's salary. She told me her attorney had secured a financial award so great she would never suffer financially after the divorce. She broke down in tears, however, when she told me her fiancé had just called off the marriage they had been planning for the past year. According to the law, where they were planning to live, her fiancé could not secure a pre-nuptial agreement to protect him from paying child support to her two minor children in the event their marriage failed. She was devastated. She told me she "was sick to the pit of her stomach" this fellow would not marry her without the agreement. She claimed she would never seek child support from him. I tried to console her but could not help but understand how this poor fellow was feeling. He lived through one divorce and was paying child support to his own kids. Paying more child support would put him over the edge. Sure it was a trust issue, but let's face it, this guy was scared. Most importantly, he was unable to move on with his life because the law afforded him no legal protection. This was a sad situation for both of them.

Another client told me how happy he was in his second marriage. That is, until his ex-wife made an application in court to have his kid's child support increased based on the argument that he and his new wife were now filing a joint tax return showing a higher income.

One of my closest friends told me, just a couple of years after my wife and I had divorced, how excited he was to be getting out of his unhappy marriage. Despite my attempts to convince him divorce may not be the best solution to his marital problems, he was convinced he would be happier without her and divorce was the only option. Three years later and attorney fees approaching the six-figure mark, he and his ex have still not settled. There won't be any new beginnings in his life for some time, if at all.

Another client, who I had known for some time, told me she was divorcing her husband of 12 years. Her husband had been suffering from stress for the past few years and was on disability leave from work. The previous year her mother had died and I really wondered how she could handle the stress of a divorce right after the death of her mother. She and her sister inherited a substantial sum of money from her mother's estate. Rather than keeping her inheritance in a separate bank account from her husband, she merged all her inheritance money into joint accounts with her husband. I was not aware that she had done this. Despite my efforts to convince her to attempt to work things out with her husband, she told me she was committed to this divorce. Perhaps she should have listened to me because she was ordered by the court to split all of their joint bank accounts, which included all the money her mother had left her. In addition, she was ordered to pay her ex-husband spousal support until he could return to work. She told me she cries every night about how terrible her life has become.

I will never forget the divorced client who made a will leaving everything to his ex-wife. He and his ex could not live together, yet according to my client, they still cared for each other very much. Having seen thousands of clients in my practice, I thought I had heard it all until this fellow came along. His story was remarkable. After he got divorced, he dated and had several short term relationships. His ex-wife had similar experiences. After nearly 10 years of dating other people they both came to the realization they were a perfect match for each other — they just couldn't live with one another. He told me, "his divorce did not mark the end of the relationship with his wife — it marked the beginning of a new relationship with his former wife."

As an attorney, I have heard many of the arguments put forward in favor of divorce. Here are a few of the most common ones:

- I have met someone else who truly understands me
- I was too young when I got married
- We have nothing in common anymore
- We have grown apart
- We fight all the time. It is hurting the kids
- I will be happier once I'm divorced
- My friends and family think a divorce is the best option

Sound familiar? Convinced these arguments are valid? Read on.

"I have met someone else who truly understands me"

Many of my clients have justified their separation by telling me they met someone else, usually followed with the comment that the new person in their life, unlike their current partner, ' understands them.' Compelling and convincing? Sure, but only if you look at one side of the argument, which is what often happens with those who leave their marriage for someone else. Let me explain.

Those who become romantically involved with someone outside the marriage are not looking at the big picture. That new person in their life does, in fact, understand them because they have nothing better to do than focus all their attention on them. That new person is always pleasant and may be satisfying a sexual need absent in their marriage. What the person who buys into this argument fails to realize is, that although the new relationship might last for some time, it will never remain at the level it was when it first began and before long, the issues that arose in the first marriage will eventually re-surface in the new one. Add an angry ex-spouse and dysfunctional children and the second relationship makes the first one look easy. I am not claiming this happens all the time, but from what I have witnessed, it happens more often than not.

"I was too young when I got married _ we have nothing in common anymore _ we have grown apart"

Those who believe their marriage will function with little or no effort are setting themselves up for failure. This goes for whomever you are married to. So before you make the decision to throw away your marriage, think about what your expectations are of that marriage. I don't care much for the popular cliché of "working on your marriage" because a successful marriage should not require work but should be filled with spark and vitality. Stop feeding a plant and it will die. Stop feeding yourself and you will die. Stop nurturing a marriage and it will die. Those who claim they have grown apart and convince themselves they made a bad decision to marry because they got married too young, in my opinion, are often using this argument to justify a more deep-rooted problem. I recently saw a client who told me she and her husband "just don't connect anymore" claiming she got married too young. I asked her what her expectations of a good marriage were. She told me a marriage should be fun. After convincing her a marriage cannot always be fun, she began rhyming off her expectations of what makes for a good marriage. I asked her if she had ever shared these expectations with her husband. She admitted she had not because, until I had posed the question, she really had not formulated in her own mind what she considered to be the attributes of a good marriage. After she left my office, she and her husband discussed their expectations and are still together.

When children are involved, I have difficulty accepting the argument that "we have nothing in common anymore – we have grown apart." Witnessing your children growing up together, on a full time basis, in my opinion, is probably the most common and most precious thing a couple can have in common. I speak from experience when I say children can strain the most solid of relationships. Children bring joy to a couple but they can also draw a couple apart because they often become the focal point of the relationship. It's great to be focused on the kids, but not at the expense of losing focus on each other.

Finally, when children are involved, do you really have the "moral" right to make the unilateral decision to end the marriage at the expense of your own happiness? Absent abuse, my position is when you chose to have the kids you gave up that right. Call me a traditionalist but a promise is a promise. And, if you made that promise and break it, what value does that promise have if you make it to the next person whom you fall in love with and promise to be with forever? You may think this argument is hard nosed but I still have not heard a valid counter argument to this one yet.

"We fight all the time. It is better for the kids to be raised in a divided home rather than a home filled with strife and unhappiness."

This is the argument that troubles me the most, especially after seeing first hand the emotional damage separation has on children. I have met many individuals who decide to separate for whatever reason and convince themselves that "it's much better if the children grow up in a divided home not one filled with strife and tension." I have great difficulty with this argument since it assumes the children will be happier living in a divided home. Let me tell you from personal experience. Children don't want a mommy in one home and a daddy in another home. Furthermore, kids don't like to be passed around from one home to another every other weekend. When my kids are with me they cry they want their mommy and daddy together under one roof, not two. If you grew up in a home with two parents, like I did, before you take the step to separate imagine how traumatic and sad it must be to be forced to live in a dysfunctional home. Is that what you want for your children? My response to mommy and daddy's who fight all the time is simple – stop it! Don't run away from the difficulties in your marriage. Confront and deal with them so you can avoid the damage it is doing to you and to your children. Live up to the promise you made of "till death do us part."

I will never forget the first time I had access to my kids for the weekend after my wife and I had separated. We went to a restaurant and the first thing my 6 year old said to me as we sat down to eat was "daddy you can sit here, mommy can sit there and we will sit across from you." I have to tell you that incident brought tears to my eyes then as it does now.

Another incident that comes to mind is a client who was a child of divorce. He told me for many years he believed he was the cause of his parents divorce. His advice to me was to always tell my kids that mom and dad love them and to assure them the divorce was not their fault. I took his advice and learned my eldest daughter believed she was the cause of our divorce. Children are not affected by divorce? Think again.

"Once I am divorced I will be happier – all my friends who are divorced are happy"

Another popular argument I hear from my clients is "many people that are divorced are happy." Perhaps they are and perhaps they are not. In my forty plus years on this earth I have learned things are not always what they seem to be. We never know what is truly going on in someone's mind do we? Many of my clients have confided to me that if they had to do it all over again they would not have divorced. They truly were unhappy in their marriage, but after they started the separation process, they were in so deep that they had to maintain a stiff upper lip and carry through with their decision. Others told me, at the time, they were so overwhelmed by the difficulties in their marriage they really did not look down the road at what impact separation and divorce would have on them and their children. Many told me they looked at their friends who were divorced and they seemed to be happy.

Beware the advice of misguided friends and family

Many of my clients have told me they sought out the advice of friends and family to assist them in making the decision to end their marriage. Be careful. It is important to remember your friends and family may be hearing only one side of the argument. Secondly, they may be too emotionally attached to you to give objective advice. What you believe is sound advice may, in fact, be misguided advice. If you take someone's advice, it is very important to understand they are not the ones who will have to live with the decision – you are!

Divorce is serious business and can, at first glance, be very seductive. Beware of the seduction of divorce.

Re-Marriage Second (or third, or fourth ...) Time Around
(Taking the plunge again – sink or swim?)

If you are separated or divorced, I'll bet you have said to yourself, "I'll never get married again." Then all of a sudden Cupid strikes. You're in love and you've got that loving feeling. You feel you are missing something because you are not married.

If you have that feeling, you are not alone. Many people who are divorced decide to re-marry. The problem is approximately sixty percent of those people end up getting divorced again.

When you get married for the first time you do so as a single person with little or no baggage. The second time around is always different. The second time around there is emotional and financial baggage and, if you or your partner have children, the children are an issue all to themselves. From what I have heard from many of my clients, one of the major reasons that many second marriages fail is because people jump in headfirst without looking. They proceed into their new relationship without learning from past relationships. I've spoken to many of my clients who have re-married. Here is what some of them had to say about second marriages.

• The False Assumption that the "experience" of having been married once will make for a successful second marriage

Many of my clients who have been married and divorced more than once have told me the experience of being married did not necessarily help them in their subsequent marriages. According to one client, being married once was not a "training course" for her second marriage. She told me, once the honeymoon was over, what she thought she had escaped from when her first marriage ended, re-appeared. She decided to re-marry because this time, unlike in her first marriage, she was in love. Unfortunately, she quickly learned love does not pay the bills and is not always sufficient to settle the everyday problems found in any relationship.

One of my clients told me she married a second time because after having been married once, she was convinced she really knew what she wanted in a partner. Unfortunately, she was blinded by love and ended up marrying a man who turned out to be worse than her first husband. Her second husband drank, gambled and turned out to have a terrible temper. She told me she did not see these character flaws until it was too late. She also told me the reason she left her first husband was because he was a "neat freak." After crying about how unhappy she was, she told me she wished her second husband was only half as good as her first husband. I'll never forget her parting words, "I didn't know what I had."

One of my clients used his experience from his first marriage in a positive way. Before he decided to tie the knot a second time, he and his second wife made a list of what they liked and disliked in their previous marriages. They then discussed how they would deal with problematic issues. He told me this exercise was a "dress rehearsal" for what was to come. In this way, he said, they knew exactly what they were in for. They both did not want any major surprises. They must have done something right. When they told me this, they had just reached a milestone anniversary and were using the occasion to make a new will.

• Sharing Life with a partner again

Speaking from experience, after you separate, you tend to assume an entirely new lifestyle. You quickly learn what it is like to be on your own again. You no longer have to account to a partner for the things you do. Being single again means you can buy what you want, go where you want, eat where and what you want and spend your free time as you wish. Before you rush into another relationship, think very carefully. Do you really want another legal partner in your life?

One of my clients left me with this positive thought about sharing her life with a new partner. Her first husband passed away when he was in his early 40s. She said he was a great guy yet she would often pick fights with him over trivial matters. She broke down as she described how tough she was on him. She said, looking back, that she was an immature spouse. She was unhappy with their marriage because she expected too much of her husband. For many years after her first husband passed away, she remained single. In her early 60s she met and married someone who had been divorced for some time. She told me she learned a valuable lesson from her first marriage. The key to a successful marriage, she maintains, is to have realistic expectations of each other. It upsets her she did not have more realistic expectations in her first marriage.

• Re-marrying because of Loneliness

If you have been divorced for some time you may be experiencing what some people refer to as, "the lonely bug." People under the spell of this bug are tired of making all decisions on their own, watching television alone, or dining out alone. If you are experiencing the "lonely bug," be careful. From what I have heard, it is not a good idea to re-marry someone just for companionship. One of my clients told me about her son who had recently divorced for the second time. She noted after his first divorce he was very upbeat. In fact, he cherished his regained "freedom." After months of going out with his buddies the novelty of being single again started to lose its luster. She told me he started to complain about being all alone in the world and that many of his friends were getting married or re-married. She told me he did not want to be the "last man left standing." So he met a lady and within a couple of months he married her and several months later they were separated. He married this lady because he was determined not to be alone. Obviously, he re-married for the wrong reason.

• A Family in a Blender – Coping with Children

From what I have heard from many clients, one of the biggest challenges that face any couple in a second marriage is dealing with children (his, hers and ours).

If children are a part of your new relationship, don't assume everything will carry on like a first — time married family with kids.

Before you commit yourself to a subsequent marriage you must realize you are not only marrying the person but their child or children as well.

Ask yourself the following: Are you going to be able to handle this new situation? What do I mean? Do you like the children? Do they like you? Are you just an outsider who is going to be living with their mother or father? How do they treat you? If they treat you poorly before you get married, have you thought about how they will treat you when you become their "stepmother/father?" What role does your new spouse expect you to assume with respect to his/her children? Do they expect you to play an active role in their upbringing or take a back seat? If you have children, will they treat your new spouse as part of the family or as an outcast?

When it comes to adult children, the situation can become even more complex. I am aware of many instances where adult children have become estranged from their parents after they re-married. I've heard many stories of jealousy, greed and personality conflicts to name but a few.

These are all issues that should be discussed before getting re-married. After you are married, it may be too late.

I've heard a number of comments from my friends and clients who re-married and created a blended family. Some of them re-married at a young age and had younger children and others re-married in their golden years when their children were adults. Here is what some of them had to say:

• "My wife's children lived with us and my kids lived most of the time with my ex-wife. Once we were married, my kids could not accept my new wife's children hugging me and calling me "daddy." I never anticipated that this would be a problem for my children but it turned out to be a big problem. As time went on, I did not know how to react to her children showing me affection in front of my kids. Since I could see that it was an uncomfortable situation for my kids, I started to show less attention to her children when my kids were around. Her kids then began to pull away from me. I never imagined that this would drive a wedge through our new family, but it did."

• "I have joint custody of my 10-year-old daughter. I am married for the second time and I have a son with my new wife. My son is 2 years old. When we were dating my second wife really seemed to bond with my daughter. Since our son was born, my wife pays little, if any, attention to my daughter. My new wife's whole world revolves around our son. On the other hand, my whole world revolves around my daughter and our son. I am really worried this is going to affect my daughter as she grows up. It is a constant source of tension in our home. It has even come to the point that if my wife doesn't stop treating my daughter as an outsider, I may consider separating from her."

• "In our first marriage my husband and I always had separate bank accounts. Somehow, this made us feel like we were separate and apart. Something was missing from our relationship. We never felt like a team. In fact, it was this lack of team spirit that ended up driving us to separate. My new spouse and I vowed everything we owned would be ours, not mine and his. We did not sign a marriage contract and everything we owned, we owned as a couple. We each have a child from our previous marriages. My child has a learning disability and requires private tutoring and a great deal of attention. My husband's child is an academic whiz and does well at school. I was shocked when, out of the blue, my husband commented we are spending a great deal of our savings to help my daughter. He told me, the more we spent to help my daughter, the less we would have to fund his child's college education. This proved to me that it was idealistic to think that we could pool all our assets even though we each had our own children with different needs."

• "My second wife's son could not accept the fact his parents got divorced. I do not have any children. My wife's son is rebellious in school and at home. He has little respect for his teachers, his mother or me. My wife does not believe in disciplining him because she feels guilty about the divorce and believes his problems will improve with time. I disagree with my wife and believe her son needs strict discipline now. I have a problem. He is not my son and he never fails to remind me of this fact. My wife and I constantly argue about this. I am at my wit's end since his behavior rules our lives and turns our house upside down. When I attempt to give him advice, my wife tells me to "back off" and leave him alone. I do not know how much more I can take."

• "Before we got married for the second time we thought we had all the bases covered. We discussed money. Paying the bills. Whose house we would live in. We even went to the extent of discussing what newspaper and magazines we would subscribe to. Somehow we forgot to talk about child rearing and routines. As it turned out, my first wife passed away and I ended up with sole custody of my son. When my son and I moved into my second wife's home with her two children, I had a rude awakening. I never realized that our views on child rearing were so different. I believe dinners should be a family affair and should take place in the dining room. My wife doesn't share my view. In fact, she allows her kids to eat dinner whenever and wherever they want. She also does not have a clean up policy. Her kids leave their dishes and clothes all over the place and she picks up after them.

I have always told my son that we should eat together as a family. Furthermore, I have always encouraged him to clean up after himself. My wife and I cannot seem to agree on this issue. It causes tension. My son feels that I am too strict with him and not strict enough with my wife's kids. I tell him I cannot be strict with my wife's kids because they are not my children. I never saw this as a problem until I was re-married."

• "My father got re-married many years after he and my mother divorced. He was the owner of a successful retail store and had substantial assets. My sister and I always felt dad lived and worked for his two kids. One year when he was on a vacation he met a woman my sister and I did not approve of. From what we saw, the woman appeared to be only interested in our father's money. My father did not see it that way. Dad told us she gave him the companionship he hadn't had for many, many, many years. Before they married, my sister and I urged my father to see a family law lawyer and get a pre-nuptial agreement. My dad would not hear of it. He was from the old school and did not believe in pre-nuptial agreements. He told us even though his marriage to our mother had failed, this woman was different. He was in love and they would never part until death. Unfortunately, when dad passed away we discovered dad really believed in what he had said. His will left everything he owned to his new wife in the belief that she would, in the end, take care of us. Well, my sister and I have had a falling out with our stepmother and we do not talk. My sister and I believe this woman, who dad thought was so special, is going to leave everything, including our dad's possessions, to her own children. It devastates my sister and me to think that dad's war medals, his uniform, his flight wings and his antique collection will probably be passed on to another family."

• "It is a second marriage for the two of us. I had a child in my first marriage who passed away. I was a broken man. I was lucky to find my second wife who has a son. He is like my own son. He even calls me "dad." He is married and has two children of his own. They call me "grandpa." During the holidays our home is filled with happiness and love. I am in my late 70s and  unfortunately my health is failing. My stepson telephones me everyday and takes me to my doctor appointments. I love him like my own son. I am very fortunate to have my family."

If you are thinking about a second marriage you may wish to look into some practical and legal issues. For example:

• You and your future spouse should talk about issues related to your finances. For instance, you should inquire as to whether your future partner has any debts, has declared bankruptcy, has any judgments registered against them and determine their credit history. It is important to know this information before naming your spouse as a joint owner on any of your assets. It is equally important to know this information before acting as a guarantor on any new financial ventures your spouse may be getting involved in. If you don't, you may be on the hook for your partner's debts.

• You and your future spouse should fully disclose all financial obligations you have to any former spouse and your children. Just because you are re-married does not mean these financial obligations go away. In fact, if your spouse has such financial obligations, they will most likely continue after their death. For your protection, you may want to find out if your future partner has arranged for insurance to pay off any debts or obligations owing at the time of his/her death.

• In most jurisdictions, debts survive death. This means if your spouse passes away the debts don't go away just because they died.

• You and your future partner should be open about what you both earn and what you both own at the time of marriage. It is always a good idea to make a list of all the assets you both own at the date of marriage and own after marriage, just in case....

• See a family law lawyer to determine what your legal obligations are regarding your new spouse and any stepchildren. For example, in some jurisdictions if you treat a stepchild like your own child, you may be on the hook for child support in the event of separation.

• Seriously consider signing a pre-nuptial agreement. A pre-nuptial agreement can protect you and your children. It can establish what your financial obligations will be to your new spouse in the event of separation or death. As previously mentioned, a pre-nuptial should be signed before the marriage when your bargaining power is strongest. It is unfortunate that many second married couples fail to recognize the importance of signing a pre-nuptial agreement to fully protect their own children. From my experience, I can tell you I see many second married couples who are shocked to learn that, without a pre-nuptial agreement, they do not have a free hand in leaving their assets to whom they wish in their will. As a matter of fact, the laws, where you live, may put your second spouse ahead of your children when it comes to leaving your assets in your will. In some jurisdictions, if you have not signed a pre-nuptial agreement, your second spouse will gain an automatic half interest in a home that you bring into the marriage and live in with that spouse. This means you would not be able to leave the entire value of that home to your children on your death. You should speak to a lawyer about the family law legislation in your area.

• Speak to a wills lawyer about second marriage will planning. It is not as simple as the first time around. You may have children from your first marriage and your spouse may have children from his/her first marriage. In a first marriage, it is common to make a will where you leave everything to your spouse and then everything to the kids. This is a risky path to follow in a second marriage. If your second spouse inherits everything you own when you die, there is nothing preventing that spouse from making a new will after you die and leaving everything you worked so hard for to his/her own children, totally cutting your children out. As a wills lawyer, I can tell you this really does happen. If you want to protect your second spouse and the children from your first marriage, you may consider leaving part of your estate to your second spouse and part of your estate to your children. This strategy will enable the children from your first marriage to benefit from your estate without having to depend upon the goodwill of your second spouse. As a further consideration in such an arrangement, you may choose to appoint a neutral party to assume the role of the executor in your will. This neutral party will ensure the best interests of your second spouse and your children will be looked after when you pass away. For example, this neutral party will decide if such assets as your cottage or business will be sold or retained.

• Prior to getting married again, take stock of all your assets and review the designations that you made on those assets. For example, you may have had your first spouse as a beneficiary on your pension plan or on your retirement savings plan. It is always wise to speak to your accountant, financial planner and lawyer prior to making any beneficiary designations.

"Your Tips"
My Legal / Financial Tips

Before Marriage – "Your Tips"

• Don't just enter into a marriage. Prepare for marriage.

• Where we live, the government discounts the fee for a marriage license if you take a marriage course. Since instituting this program, divorces have been on the decline. This course gave my wife and I a solid foundation to build upon.

• You should communicate with your life partner like you would with a potential business partner. Hammer out the tough issues before you commit. Don't forget to discuss issues like:
– where you will live;
– will both of you work;
– children? If so, how many?
– the contingency plan if one of your parents get sick and needs someone to care for them;
– etc.

• When I met my husband, one of the first things I noticed was his great sense of humor. That quality has helped us get through the tough times.

• In the world of physics opposites attract but in the world of marriage if there is not much in common, opposites soon lose their attraction.

• Don't forget your friends. You'll want them after you are married. Be careful not to lose them before you are married.

• My husband and I always showed appreciation to our future in-laws for all the things they did for us before we got married. This helped to set the tone for a warm relationship after we got married.

• Even though you are an adult, it does not hurt to listen to your parents and others who care for you.

My Legal/Financial Tips
Before The Marriage

• Don't be afraid to talk about money before you get married and commit to continuing this discussion throughout the marriage – Money is one of the major causes of marital breakdown.

• Enter into the relationship with full disclosure about each other's assets and debts. A pre-nuptial agreement, prepared by an attorney, will ensure you both have full disclosure of each other's assets and liabilities.

• To find out more about each other's attitudes towards money, consider playing the "What Am I Worth Today?" game. On a piece of paper, set out two headings —"What I Own Today" and "What I Owe Today." Under the heading "What I Own Today", list what you own. Don't limit the list to what you have in cold cash. List it all, including the personal stuff like your car, television and other personal items remembering to give each item an estimated value (remember most items purchased lose their value once you take them out of the store or off the car lot). By the way, potential inheritances don't count. It's not yours yet, if at all.

On the other side of the page, list what you owe. What you owe might include credit card debts, student loans, loans made to you by family or friends, income taxes owed and accumulated interest, etc. Your partner must do the same.

If at the end of the game you find out that you own more than you owe but your future partner owes more than they own, you may have won the game but you may end up being the loser in the long term.

If your future partner owes more than he/she owns, before you get married, you may be marrying a person with little or no financial responsibility. In fact, after marriage, you may end up using what you own to pay off what he/she owes.

A word of caution, don't ever assume that marriage will turn a financially irresponsible person into a financially responsible spouse.

You cannot necessarily take the results of the game at face value. Your future partner may have a valid reason for owing more than they own. For example, your potential spouse may have spent a fortune on tuition fees at dental school but will quickly make it up in future earnings.

• A poor credit rating could have a negative impact on the financial stability of your marriage. For example, if one of you has a poor credit rating you may end up paying a higher interest rate at the bank when borrowing money for a family car and/or house. More importantly, a poor credit rating may be a warning sign that one of you is not financially responsible.

• Seriously consider meeting with a family law attorney to determine the legal effect(s) a common law relationship or marriage will have before you take the plunge. A family law attorney will be able to advise you on how to protect the things you own if the relationship goes sour.

• In some jurisdictions, marriage will void any will made before the date of marriage. This means you will have to make a new will after you get married.

• Discuss where you see yourselves financially in 5, 10, 15, etc. years. Will you own a home? Will you forego home ownership for travel and leisure? Are you and your spouse concerned about retirement planning? If children are being planned for, are you going to fund their college or will that be their responsibility?

• Are both of you willing to live according to a mutually agreeable budget? A budget will work only if both of you are willing to follow it. If you are a "live by a budget" kind of person and your partner isn't, make sure that their commitment to a budget is genuine and not just a way of smoothing over a difficult topic before the marriage.

• Keep a record of all assets you bring into the marriage. It is best to do this as close as possible to the marriage date. Put your records in a safe place where your new spouse cannot access them. Why? In most jurisdictions, assets acquired before marriage are exempt from net family property. The only way you can prove what you brought into the marriage is if you have records.

• Keep a record of gifts given to you personally during the marriage. In most jurisdictions, gifts acquired after marriage (made in your name) are generally excluded from net family property. This means the gift will not have to be shared with your spouse in the event the marriage should fail. For example, if your parents give you a gift of money and you keep that money in your own bank account (in your name only) and the marriage should fail, that money will not have to be shared with your ex-spouse. If however, you place that money in a joint bank account with your spouse or use it to pay off the mortgage on the family home, you will, most likely, have to share it with your ex.

During The Marriage/Living Together
"Your Tips"

• I wish today I had invested my cash wedding gifts instead of squandering the money on frivolous things.

• Be yourself. If something is bothering you, tell your spouse. Don't walk on "eggshells." Confront your concerns.

• Negativity in a marriage translates into unhappiness. Do whatever it takes to turn a negative into a neutral or whenever possible, a positive. Negativity is contagious.

• Remember the word appreciation and don't forget to show it. Treat your spouse like any other person who does something nice for you.

• It's not a problem to admit you are wrong. The words, "I'm sorry," "It is my fault" can go a long way.

• When you got engaged he/she was that special person to you. Once married, don't forget you married that special person. Always remember to treat that person in a special way.

• Things are not always what they appear. I thought my husband and I were the only couple having problems. Funny thing, we are still together but our friends, who always appeared happy, are now divorced.

• I make a habit of saying something nice to my partner everyday.

• Remember you do not own your partner. Being alone once in a while and doing things without your partner is OK. In fact, it can refresh the relationship.

• I've always linked marriage to driving a car. The drive is not always down a one way street. When you begin the trip you have to prepare. You look at a map and you start off slow. It is important to not be afraid to ask for directions from people who have taken the trip and are familiar with the smooth open roads along with the detours and the potholes. Sometimes you have to yield and give your partner a break. Other times you have to stop and change direction. Always remember to check behind you and see where you came from and to remember were the road hazards were. Accept the fact that even though you begin the trip in sunshine, there will inevitably be inclement weather along the way.

• Don't use double talk. Be open and honest with your spouse, otherwise, you may inadvertently create suspicion. For example, whenever I went out for dinner with a co-worker, I always told my wife. If my dining companion was a female, I made it clear where we were going and that she was welcome to attend, if she wished.

• Keep disagreements between yourselves. Make every effort not to discuss your differences with your parents or family. Once things have been said, they cannot be taken back. Once attitudes about a person are formed, they are rarely forgotten.

• When times get rough, my husband and I make a point of reminding ourselves about the reasons we fell in love in the first place. We focus on what is good about our marriage, not on what is bad. We have just celebrated our 35th wedding anniversary.

• Love is as fragile as a fine piece of china and should always be treated with care. I came to this realization after my first marriage failed. When the infatuation ends people are not as careful about what they say or do. My second wife and I are very careful about what we say and how we act towards one another. Our guard is never down. This has been the secret of our long and happy marriage — 25 years.

• Think before you speak. Words once spoken, can never be taken back.

• Children are a blessing to any marriage but should not compete with your needs as a couple. We learned very early in our marriage to take time for each other every two weeks. We pre-booked a baby sitter for every second Friday night. At first the kids complained and gave us the guilt trip but eventually they looked forward to having Sally (the babysitter) spend time with them.

• People ask me how I knew Jason was the one — my answer is simple. I knew he was the one when I said "I do."

My Legal/Financial Tips
During The Marriage/Living Together

• When you are married, it is important to think about protecting one another in case of illness, disability or death. If one of you becomes sick and/or disabled and unable to work or worse yet dies, will there be enough money to care for your spouse and children? Speak to an insurance agent about critical illness, disability and life insurance.

• If, prior to the marriage, you had existing life insurance, retirement plans and/or pension plans, you should review those plans and consider revising the beneficiary on those plans. On your review you may find that your mother and father are the named beneficiaries. Now that you are married, you may wish to name your spouse as the beneficiary.

• Speak to your accountant and lawyer about the tax benefits and ramifications of making your spouse the beneficiary of retirement savings plans and any assets that have capital growth.

• If you or your spouse are involved in a business, you should review any partnership or shareholder agreements that may be in place. You may be surprised to learn that the agreement may limit your ability to leave your interest in the partnership or shares in the company to your spouse in a will. Many such agreements often specify that the spouse of the partner or shareholder is not entitled to be involved in the company after the death of the spouse but rather, is only entitled to a monetary pay out.

If you are involved in a company and your business partner is about to be married, this may be the time to discuss a partnership or shareholder agreement with your business partner, otherwise, on his or her death you may find his or her spouse is now your new business partner. Such agreements can be of value in the event of marital breakdown as well as death.

• Make a budget and live by it. Your budget however, should be realistic. It is important to have enough 'give and flexibility' to make it work. A budget should never put you into a financial prison, which can cause tension in the relationship. You may have an impulse urge to buy that "gotta have" power tool. How are you going to feel if your spouse says that 'it is not part of our budget?' Or that weekend shopping trip with your friends. How would you feel if you have to tell your friends you cannot go because you and your spouse are on a strict budget? Here is a suggestion. If you are intent on having a strict budget, why not take the middle ground? You and your spouse could each have a bank account with fun money that you can spend as you please without having to account to the other.

• Decide who is going to pay the bills and handle the finances. It is best if both of you are involved. I have witnessed many widows and widowers who become totally lost when it comes to bills and finances because their spouse always handled these matters.

• Keep records of the location of bank accounts, investments, benefits, etc.. It is also a good idea to know when your credit card and other bills are due. This way you won't miss paying them on time.

• Be up front with each other about the location and extent of your assets. Millions of dollars are lost each year by people who pass away without having disclosed their assets to their spouse or immediate family.

• Be up front about your debts. Some of my clients have told me they have run credit checks on their future spouses to see what they were getting into. For some, it was a wise decision.

• Caution: Be careful of debt. Borrow reasonably and ensure that you can manage the debt. One of my clients once summarized what debt meant to him — **DON'T EVER BE THERE.**

• Use credit cards wisely. If you cannot control their use, consider putting them away for a rainy day. Don't cancel your credit cards because you may have to re-apply to activate them again.

• Tighten up your credit card collection. Do you really need 6 or 7 credit cards? Too many cards can lead to a financial mess. You may end up paying needless interest on an overdue account because of confusion of due dates, misplaced statements, etc..

• Pay off your credit cards during the interest free period. After that period expires the interest charged by the credit card companies is more than what a bank would charge for a consumer loan.

• If you have credit card debt that is piling up, consider visiting with a bank manager to get a bank loan to pay off those cards. This is known as a consolidation loan. Interest rates for consolidation loans are usually much lower than the rate charged by credit card companies.

• Consider visiting with your bank manager to arrange for lines of credit just in case you need funds in the future. You will always be better positioned to have the money at hand rather than arranging for funds with deadlines looming.

• There is a great deal of competition in the financial industry. Shop around for the best interest rates and terms. Just because the interest rate is good does not necessarily mean the repayment terms will be. Make sure you understand the terms of the loan.

• If you need a mortgage to buy the family home choose a mortgage that is best suited to your needs. Understand the mortgage before you sign. Choosing a mortgage that is not right for your situation can spell disaster for the family. Find out if there is a penalty associated with paying off the mortgage before the due date. Find out how much of the mortgage you can prepay every year. Find out how many payments you can make per month. A mortgage specialist and/or a real estate attorney can help you understand the terms before you sign.

• Be open with your spouse about potential financial difficulties. Some of my clients have told me they were embarrassed to tell their spouse they had been fired. In the meantime, their spouse assumed all was well and continued to spend as if they were in a two-income family.

• Make a will. Why? Because if you don't, the government decides who inherits your things and if you have children, your spouse may only get a part of what you own. Don't assume that a will is only for the rich. Everyone over the age of majority needs a will. If you assume that you have nothing because all you have is debt, don't forget about life insurance policies and group policies that only pay out when you die. Suddenly what was once an estate of debt, becomes an estate with assets.

If you have children and do not have a will, those children, in a worse case scenario, could become wards of the state. A will ensures that a guardian of your choosing immediately attends to your children.

Both you and your spouse should have your own wills.

Don't be intimidated by a will. Generally speaking, a will does not specifically list every asset you own. Think of your estate in terms of a pie. You can leave the whole pie to one person if you wish or you may decide to divide up the pie into a number of pieces and divide those pieces amongst a number of people. By approaching a will this way, no matter what you own when you die gets divided up accordingly whether you own 50 dollars or $500,000 dollars. Of course, if you wish to pick out a particular item, such as your diamond ring and leave it to a particular person such as your niece, you can do that. Similarly, if you wish to leave a sum of money to a person you can do this as well. These gifts are commonly referred to as "legacies" and come out of the pie before the pie is divided up.

If it is your intention to make a will and divide your estate among your spouse and a number of other people, the law, depending upon where you live, may provide your spouse with the right to reject that choice and claim an equalization of your family property. In other words, your spouse may be entitled to receive more than you gave him/her under the provisions of your will.

Here are a few things to consider before you meet with a lawyer to prepare your will:

• **The Executor:** Every will requires the appointment of what is commonly known as an executor. An executor looks after your estate when you die. A beneficiary in your will can also be an executor. This means that your spouse can be your beneficiary and your executor. It is important to consider who will look after your estate if both you and your spouse pass away together in a common accident. This individual or individuals are known as alternate or back-up executors. It is wise to name two different people to act in the roles of executor and guardian. In so doing, you are protecting your children from potential financial abuse by the guardian. If two different people fill those roles, the executor can keep a check on spending by the guardian.

• **Beneficiary:** A beneficiary is a person or charity who gets a gift and/or a piece of your pie. You should also have a contingency plan in place in the event the beneficiary dies before you.

• **Legal Guardian:** A legal guardian is the person you appoint to have custody of your minor children in the event you and your spouse die before your child (ren) reaches the age of majority. It is wise to consider appointing a "back-up" guardian in the event your primary guardian passes away before you do. A guardian should be someone whom you believe will care for your children and get along with them. Many of my clients have a difficult time choosing a guardian because they believe no one can replace them as parents. It is difficult to imagine someone else raising our children but this decision should not preclude you from making a will. The appointment of a guardian is one of the most important reasons for young couples to make a will.

• **A Trust:** If you have young children (under the age of majority) your will should contain a trust. A trust is simply a legal way of describing that you want your child's inheritance to be managed and invested by your executor until your child (ren) reach a specified age. An age such as, 21, 25, 30, etc.

• When you visit with your attorney to make a will, discuss the importance of a financial power of attorney. If you or your spouse become incapacitated you need someone to be able to sign financial documents on your behalf. A will only takes effect upon death. It does not give your spouse authority to act on your behalf while you are alive. If you are in a car accident and lose your mental capacity who will be able to pay your bills? Who will do your banking? Who will pay your mortgage? Who will renew your mortgage, etc.? In a financial power of attorney you can appoint someone, you trust, to act on your behalf should you become incapable. Of course you can appoint your spouse as the primary attorney but it is also wise to appoint at least one back up in the event both you and your spouse are incapacitated. It is important to know that the word "attorney" in the term "power of attorney" does not mean you have to appoint your lawyer.

If you become incapacitated without a power of attorney in place, your assets could be frozen and, depending upon where you live, your spouse may be forced to apply to the government or to the court in order to act on your behalf.

You should also speak to your attorney about a medical power of attorney to ensure that someone is able to make medical decisions on your behalf when you cannot.

"Your Tips"
Marriage Breakdown/Divorce

• I tried to be a nice guy during my separation. I did not fight and gave her everything she wanted. I wanted to remain civil. She and her lawyer saw this as a sign of weakness and I am paying for that decision to this day. If I ever have to go through this again, I will be civil, but TOUGH!

• Sometimes it is better to give in rather than fight. I spent more in legal fees over who gets the computer equipment than a new system would have cost. Heck, with the money I spent I could have bought a room full of computers and a server. Remember, it is your divorce not your lawyer's. Don't be afraid to ask how much every move is going to cost you before you decide to make it.

• Rather than hiring strangers, who really didn't have our best interests at heart, we decided to turn to our families to mediate our differences. As a matter of fact, my now ex-wife was adamant about having sole custody of our two children. If we had hired lawyers, I am sure her lawyer would have fought to the death to get her what she wanted. In our situation, by not having a stranger involved, it worked for the best interest of us all. When my ex-wife stated that she wanted sole custody of our kids, her mom and dad disagreed and told her that she was wrong to force this point and that it was in all of our interests that we both have joint and shared physical custody of our kids. The same thing with the division of our property. My parents told me how important it was for my ex-wife to get an equitable division of our property. Guess what? Even though we are divorced, we are still friends. There is no animosity or ill feelings. We are still able to talk and laugh with our ex-in-laws. Our kids see everyone on a regular basis. Most importantly, the money we saved in legal costs is now being invested for our children.

• Never take a job with your in-laws. I am divorced and now unemployed.

• Separation does not always mean you will get divorced. We didn't! We used the separation period to re-discover ourselves and learn how much more unhappy we would have been not being with each other.

• We had a turbulent marriage. I couldn't wait to get divorced. I initiated the divorce. After 3 years of wandering, dating, living with someone, I couldn't wait to re-marry him. Luckily he was still available. Sometimes, your first choice is the best.

• Divorce rips a child in half. I am speaking from experience. My parents got divorced when I was 5 years old. I am now 35. I don't buy the so-called experts that claim kids don't suffer. We do!!!

• After 19 years of marriage I am single again. Terrific? Well, not really. It is not what I expected. I never realized how much easier life is when you have someone who can help share the day to day responsibilities. I thought once I was separated it would be palm trees and pina coladas. With the way things are going, my palm trees are weeping willows and my pina colada is ice water to wash down my headache pills.

• I made the mistake of letting my emotions take control of me. I wanted revenge for what he did to me. I got the revenge but I also got my lawyer's bill and now I want revenge against my lawyer.

• All divorces are not created equal. My advice — Don't assume that your divorce will turn out like someone else's. My friend told me that her divorce hurt a little, was relatively quick and inexpensive. My divorce was not like that. She had no kids and all she had was her house.

• Don't speak ill of your former spouse to your children, no matter how old they are, even as a joke. Remember your ex-spouse is their parent and your children do not necessarily hold the same opinion of your ex-spouse as you do.

• Before you make any move during your divorce (such as, a phone call, letter or direction to your lawyer) stop, take a deep breath, think about it and think about it again a few hours later. It is important to remember your actions can set off an expensive and dangerous chain reaction.

• After you get separated, spend some time alone to take stock of where you are and where you are going. A new relationship may be pre-mature.

• Be wary of the advice of friend's and family who encourage you to separate. Their intentions may be good but consider if they really have more than your short term happiness in mind. Think about the long term ramifications separation may have on you and your kids.

My Legal/Financial Tips
Marriage Breakdown/Divorce

• Remember it takes two people to marry but only one to divide the family in half. If you have just been notified your spouse no longer wants the marriage, don't call the first family law attorney you see in the phone book. Try to get referrals from friends, family or call the local law association. Once you get some names, meet with the lawyers to determine if you can work together, what their strategy will be and get a firm estimate of what their fees will be.

• Learn about the family laws in your jurisdiction. Visit the library and speak with family and friends who have been down this road. The better informed you are, the wiser your decisions will be.

• ALWAYS REMEMBER the attorney is working for you. Do not let the attorney drive your case. A sign of a good attorney is one that presents options and lets you decide. Please read this again. I cannot emphasize how important it is to never be bullied or intimidated by your attorney. Remember you are the client and your attorney is there to serve your interests, not their own.

• If you have not already done so, make copies of all documents that will be important and relevant to your case. These documents may include such things as bank records, tax returns, investment certificates, stocks, land registration documents, etc..

• Make an inventory list of everything in your home. Take photos and videos if possible. The list, photos and videos can be invaluable if you wind up in court. It is best to take these steps while you are still in your home so you won't have to rely on your memory.

• When it comes to dividing your property between you and your spouse — play it smart. Choose wisely. For example, if you can't afford the upkeep of a cottage, don't ask for it in a settlement. You may be better off with other assets that won't cost you money to maintain.

• Set up your own individual bank accounts.

• Notify your pay and benefits department at work so they can adjust their records and offer some suggestions.

• Review and change (if you wish) the designated beneficiaries on your retirement plans, pension plans, insurance policies, investments etc.. It is likely your separated or former spouse is named as the beneficiary on these documents.

• Contact credit card companies and cancel all joint credit cards you have with your spouse. In so doing, you will not be responsible for purchases made by your separated spouse. A word to the wise. If you intend to keep your divorce amicable, notify your spouse before you cancel any joint credit cards. This can help avoid an embarrassing situation for your spouse if he/she has to use the card only to find out that it is no longer valid. The same advice applies to joint bank accounts. Don't forget to change all computer access to bank records so your spouse no longer has access to your financial information. One of my clients told me, after she separated, she was able to track all the spending habits of her ex husband because he did not change his access password. She later used that information against him in court.

• Consider establishing your own individual credit rating.

• Make a new will. Separation is not the same as divorce. If you are separated you are still considered married. In many jurisdictions, if you pass away without a will, your separated spouse could end up inheriting part of your estate, because your separated spouse is considered your legal spouse until you are divorced.

• Make new powers of attorney. Separation does not revoke your will or powers of attorney. You must take proactive steps to ensure these documents are in order.

• Take it from me, there is life after divorce no matter how bad it may look today. It may not always be happy, but life goes on. Always remember to look forward.

• Don't assume you will be happy with a person that has a complete opposite personality to your former spouse. Let me explain. My ex-husband had a temper. I went for the first guy that came along that was shy, quiet and non-reactive. The result? I am married to a whimp and a momma's boy and I am not happy.

• Really get to know your future second spouse BEFORE you make any commitment. I don't mean just what their political views are or whether they like chocolate or vanilla. I mean the real things that people have to live with day to day. Does he nag? Is she possessive? Is he demanding? Is she tidy or messy? Does he snore? Etc..

• Many of my divorced friends blame their ex-spouses for their failed marriages. I on the other hand came to the realization my ex and I were both at fault. After our divorce, I stepped back and honestly and objectively examined where I went wrong so I would not repeat those mistakes in my second marriage. Before my second marriage, I told my future husband about some of my quirks and habits, which may have not been apparent to him and asked if he could live with them. Those quirks and habits are things I know I cannot change. I just wanted him to know what they were, so he would not be surprised later on.

• As a child who grew up living with a mother, stepfather and a biological father who did not have custody of me, I can tell you that despite all the efforts on my mother's part to make us one family together with my stepfathers children, I never bought my mother's fantasy that we could live happily ever after as a "blended" family. Speaking from experience, stepfamilies are "mixed" families, not "blended" families. Stepchildren have no choice. We are forced into this situation. We have no blood ties to our stepsiblings and many of us have our biological parents who we cherish dearly. My advice to all stepchildren. Retain your individuality and be proud of who you are and where you come from. Don't feel you have to join the stepfamily team and pretend to be someone you are not.

• A healthy second marriage may be great for the spouses but not necessarily for the children. I am happy my father got remarried to a wonderful woman but it is hard for me to get over the fact my dad's new happiness came about because of a tragedy that befell our family. Every time I look at my stepmom, I cannot help but think I would not have known this woman had my mother not died in a car accident. Parents who are getting married should take this into consideration when attempting to get us to accept our stepparents. My advice to parents who are getting re-married — understand what is going on in our minds and be considerate of our feelings.

• Stepparents beware-prepare for potential minefields ahead. If you get married again, you are not just marrying your spouse but their children also. Children who have been raised a certain way. Children with established values and most importantly, children who may have problems. What kind of problems? School, behavioral, health, etc. Be prepared as a stepparent not just to be there for the good times, but also for the bad times. When the bad times roll around, don't assume you can get away with saying, "they are not my kids." If you think that you will be unable to handle this added pressure, then don't get re-married to this person.

• If you want to build trust between yourself and your stepchildren, sign a pre-nuptial agreement before you re-marry. Before I got re-married I heard whispers from my husband's children that I was marrying their father for his money. As years went by, the whispers turned into outright accusations. These feelings started to cause a division between him and his family and me. It got to the point where I was ready to call it a day. I decided to put my money where my mouth was and do the next best thing to a pre-nuptial agreement by signing a postnuptial agreement. Unfortunately, the damage has been done and my step kids and I have a very cold relationship. This could have all been avoided had we initially signed a pre-nup.

• Start your second marriage with a fresh, new attitude. Don't compare your second spouse to your first spouse, good or bad!

• I commend my wife for helping me to get to know her children because now we have a wonderful relationship. My wife just didn't toss me into the situation but rather prepared me and educated me about her kids. Without her kids knowing about it, she showed me their report cards, talked to me about what subjects they liked and didn't like. She talked about their friends and their favorite teachers. She walked me through their family albums and I got to learn where they have been and where they would like to go. Her kids really like me because I take an interest in them and know a lot about them.

My Legal/Financial Tips
Re-marriage

• I cannot over emphasize the importance of a pre-nuptial agreement in a second marriage situation. By signing a pre-nuptial agreement, you and your future spouse will know where you stand if the marriage goes bad and depending upon where you live, the pre-nuptial agreement will give you the freedom to choose who will inherit your estate. For example, if it is your intention in your will, to leave everything you own to the children of your first marriage, a pre-nuptial agreement will enable you to accomplish this goal.

• Make a new will. Depending upon where you live, if you die without a will, the law could give your new spouse your entire estate.

Also remember if you have made a will before your second marriage, in many jurisdictions, the marriage may void your existing will. This means, if you have a will leaving everything to your children from your first marriage and you get re-married, that will could be invalid. Be careful when doing second marriage will planning. Make sure you see an experienced estate attorney. Let me explain why. If you plan a second marriage will like you would a first marriage will, your estate may end up in the hands of your stepchildren and not your biological children. In a first marriage, it is common to leave everything you own to your spouse and then when your spouse dies, to your children.

Imagine using this type of planning in a second marriage situation. If you leave everything you own to your second spouse, he or she will become the owner of everything you own when you pass away. There is nothing stopping your second spouse from making a new will after you die and leaving everything he or she owns (which includes everything he or she inherited from you) to his or her own children. This means your children, from the first marriage, could inherit absolutely nothing from all your years of hard work and saving. There are a couple of options, among others, which you should talk about with your estate attorney. For example, you could leave part of your estate to your second spouse and part to your children from your first marriage. This way your children will get their inheritance without having to depend on the goodwill of your second spouse to include them in his or her will. Another alternative is to think of establishing a trust for your second spouse who allows him or her to benefit from your estate for his or her lifetime but upon his or her death your estate will be distributed to the children from your first marriage. In most jurisdictions however, you can only entertain these options if you have a marriage contract.

• Be careful of putting assets in joint names with your second spouse without first speaking with an estate attorney. Joint assets automatically transfer to your second spouse upon your death regardless of what your will says about those assets. I always tell my clients what they own jointly is not theirs to give away. The moment after you take your last breath, that joint asset is legally owned by the other joint owner or owners.

• Make a list of what you own, your spouse owns and what is owned by both of you. Put this list in a safe place so your family members know who owned what when you pass away. It is important not to be flippant when it comes to personal effects and second marriage will planning. Imagine this scenario. You pass away and in your will you leave all your personal effects to your children. Your kids come into your home and tell your second spouse they are taking all of the furniture, stereo equipment, etc. Your second spouse claims these items were purchased during the marriage by both of you. The next step could be litigation between your children and your second spouse.

• Think about the benefits of life insurance. Life insurance can be a very valuable estate planning tool in a second marriage. If your intention is to provide for your children from your first marriage as well as your second spouse, you could use life insurance in this way. Your will could leave everything you own to your children and on the other hand, a life insurance policy could benefit your second spouse.

If you have minor children from a previous marriage and you are paying child support, do not assume that the child support ends when you die. In most cases, your estate will be responsible for supporting your children. Life insurance is another way of providing for your children without depleting your estate, thereby leaving an estate for your second spouse and protecting him or her from financial ruin.

• Consider making new powers of attorney. Unlike a will, in most jurisdictions, marriage does not revoke a power of attorney.

• Consider many of the points I listed in the "marriage section" of this book such as beneficiary designations, budget, delegation of duties, etc. In second marriages, finances are often a touchy subject. Be prepared to discuss who pays for what. What comes from a joint account and what comes from your own individual accounts.

• If there are children from previous relationships, discuss how their financial needs will be looked after, such as who pays for their food, clothes, entertainment needs, etc.

• Remember to love and be kind to each other no matter what challenges you face because with second marriages there will be challenges.

His Story, Her Story, Your Story

Life Expectancy

Dear Larry:

Have glitter and gold ever overtaken you only to realize that it's not 24 carat gold but fools gold? Well that's what happened to me in a nutshell.

Ever since I can remember I was a big fan of the daily soap operas. Many times I would rush home after school to catch an episode. My day was not whole if I missed out on what happened. As a matter of fact my walls were filled with posters of my favorite star (for confidentiality reasons I will call him Lance Heartbreaker because he is well known). How many times did I wish that I could be the actress who was romantically involved with him. Oh what a hunk. Lance was the man. He was what I compared all my dates to and even to my now ex-husband. I would always think if a date did not open a door for me he was nothing like Lance who always did so on the show. Call me a hopeless romantic, but I wanted to find a man who could bring out the passion in me and make me feel like a woman.

It is terrible for me to say, but I settled for a lot less than my dream man Lance. I married Bruce, your average American guy — football, hot dogs, beer, the kids, the dog and then me. Bruce was a good husband, don't get me wrong. He always respected me, brought home his paycheck, never gambled, never drank to excess — he just fell into the married man groove. What I mean is, the kids came along and everyday was like the day before. It all changed when I saw an ad in the local paper promoting one of the stores in the mall. "Come see a soap opera heartthrob in person." I had to go. I even took off work that day. I was praying that it would be Lance. Oh the things that I wanted to say to him. When I got to the store I realized it was not Lance but another of my favorites, who I will call Spanish Love. I went up to him and shook his hand and like a teenie bopper I told him what a big fan I was and how much I loved his romanticism. He took my hand, gave me a little wink, kissed my hand and whispered in my ear he would like to drink some wine with me tomorrow over lunch. The thrill of my lifetime happened in an instant. For a moment I forgot I was married. In fact, I pinched myself to see if this was all a dream. I even told my husband about it. It was no secret. He was thrilled for me. The problem is, I only told my husband about the lunch. I never told him about the dinners and the other romantic encounters that we shared. As a matter of fact, my husband didn't know I was having an affair until I told him I was leaving. Oh, Spanish Love was a dream come true both emotionally and romantically. It was like living in a fantasy world. Dinners always in fancy restaurants. He never met me without a red rose in his hand. His Spanish accent put me in a different world. He would constantly say he loved me with that hot blooded Spanish tongue. It did not take me long to forget about beer, hot dogs, football, the kids and Bruce. I had found the love of my life. My soul mate. That is until I married Spanish Love. He really should have got an award for his acting because he was a master. You can't imagine what it feels like when your husband tells you that he wants to be able to date other women even though he is married. You also can't imagine paying his debts. His favorite number was 25 both in woman's ages and on the roulette table. Boy was I duped. But I had to smile whenever I went to parties with him. He would always whisper to me, "people are watching, smile." There were no more roses or opening car doors for me. That was reserved for TV and those 25 year olds. I was just his has been. A re-run.

Our marriage lasted 2 years. I was miserable. I lost my family. My friends think I am an idiot. As a matter of fact, my kids stopped talking to me and never want to see me. I am so lonely and embarrassed. I can't believe I could have been so stupid.

Larry, people who live life in a fantasy world should be wary.

Love On The Line

Dear Larry:
Heard you on the radio last night and just had to email you. You spoke about how awkward and difficult it is to meet somebody second time around. I wish I would have heard you about 4 years ago and listened to your advice. Here's my story.

My wife left me and she has custody of my 2 kids who live in a different city. I don't see them very much. Frankly, I am very lonely. I am only in my late 30's and feel I got really ripped off by my ex. Hey, I was a family man and missed the female companionship and the kids. Six months after we separated, I decided to get back into the dating game. I was married for over 15 years and was very scared. I had never been with another woman other than my wife. We were both virgins. I didn't know where to start so I asked all of my friends if they knew anyone they could fix me up with. I had lots of dates, but nothing worked out. Blind dates were a disaster. I started to wonder if there were any women that I was compatible with. This went on for about a year. I then decided there had to be a way of "weeding out" incompatibility. So I decided to join an internet dating service. I was a little leery at first because I am not that adept on the computer. But I finally got the courage to do it. I spent the $40 per month and filled out the profile — who I am, my habits, my characteristics, my likes, my dislikes, my age, what I thought would be the perfect mate, what I thought would be the perfect first date and what I wanted — a date, a long term relationship or marriage. It is a dating resume. I couldn't help but think as I was completing it that no one was verifying that what I was putting down was accurate and honest. Larry, I am an honest guy, but let me tell you some of the people out there are not honest. Many, I found, lied about their weight, their age and their interests. After I signed on, I was like a kid in a candy store. I would spend hours looking at the women on the site. On the first night, I emailed 10 women who interested me. The next day, I couldn't wait to get up to go to my computer at work and see how many women responded to me. Larry, I didn't get one email. I received 15. Those 10 women I emailed were very interested and gave me their phone numbers and the other 5 wanted my telephone number. I didn't know who to call first. I work in a clerical job, so I decided the best thing to do right off the bat was open a file on each one. In the file I listed the lady's telephone number, when I called, what I said and where I was taking them. After each date, I went back to the file and made notes about what we talked about, what she liked and didn't like and when I was supposed to call her next. I have to say I was having a great time. It cost me a fortune of money and almost cost me my job. What happened was my boss caught me emailing the ladies on company time. Ironically, he is divorced too and now he is hooked. During lunch hour we surf together. One time we even fought over a pretty face on the net. Naturally, I gave in because he is my boss. Funny how life is, Larry, that date turned out to be a fraud. Instead of being 35, she turned out to be 55. Back to my tale. What you tend to forget, is that the people on the computer are in fact people with feelings and emotions. To me, it became a game — like a man on the hunt. It was also a very expensive game. Those dates were fun but they were emptying my bank account. It got so bad, that I could barely pay the rent and the child support. Not only that, I started to lose control. The women would call me to get together and I am a guy that can't say no. The problem was my game plan did not contemplate the women calling me. So when they called if I didn't have my file beside me, I began to get confused about who was who. In fact, I started calling Carol, Denise (not a great way to build a relationship). I realized what a foolish and manipulative person I had become when my notes in my file were lost. I didn't know who was who, when I was supposed to call, who I was supposed to call. I was a man in a maze. I am sure I hurt a lot of people. I really feel bad. You know, Larry, it wasn't until I lost the file that I stopped. If not, I would probably still be on that site hurting other people. Larry tell your audience to not get caught up in the web.

A Child's Cry For Help

Dear Larry:
I have two kids who live with my ex-wife. I have been divorced for 3 years now and it was a bitter divorce. I have visitation and telephone privileges, but it is obviously not enough for my 8-year-old daughter because she has to sneak a call to me when her mother is not in the room. This is happening more and more and I don't know what to do. I can hear the pain in her voice. "Daddy, when are you coming back?" "Why aren't you together with mommy?" "How far away is next weekend when I get to see you?" "I pray every night that God will bring you back." It breaks my heart. The tears are welling up as I write this to you. When she was born, I was the first person to hold

her. I vowed this child would not be part of a broken home like I came from. I am afraid of what this is doing to her. Can you believe a child has to be so devious that she has to call her daddy behind her mommy's back. I would never have dream't that MY child would have to go through this at such a young age. I never dream't that I would have to speak to my child in this clandestine way. What a tragedy.

Food For Thought

Dear Larry:

When my wife and I met, we were both over weight. I weighed 350 pounds and my wife weighed 300 pounds. Looking back on when we first met, I believe the only thing we had in common was our weight — people made fun of us but we did not make fun of each other.

After being married for about 5 years, I woke up one day and decided that I did not want to live like this – I did not like the way I looked. My doctor advised that I was a ticking time bomb. I started to take an interest in losing weight. I subscribed to fitness magazines, joined a gym and hired a personal trainer. I started going to the gym once a week because I was very self-conscious about being in the midst of so many fit people. As my weight dropped off, I began to go to the gym more often. Now I'm going everyday. It is a big part of my life. Larry — I have lost over 150 pounds and I feel like a new person. The problem is, my wife has no interest in exercising and losing weight. She says this is the way the creator made her and this is the way she is going to be. It is amazing but I feel like I am married to a stranger now. We are so different than when we tied the knot. I love my family. But the ironic thing is she mocks me for acting like a kid. She makes fun of me in front of my friends because I like to go blading near the beach. My wife claims my new healthy lifestyle is nothing more than a middle age crisis. She say's I am acting like I am 24 not 44. She thinks I am doing this so I can meet a cute chick with a firm body. In reality, this is not my intention. Shouldn't she be happy that her husband is healthier and emotionally more balanced? It's as if she is jealous of me. And I don't care for some of the embarrassing remarks that she is throwing at me lately. I never embarrass her for not exercising so why should she embarrass me for exercising? How do we get things back to the way they were? Should I stop exercising or should I just keep trying to convince her to take up the lifestyle?

Financial Low Flyer

Can you help me Larry? I'm just about to grab my parachute and bailout. I am losing patience with my ace pilot husband.

When I met Mike, he was a first officer for a major airline. I met him on a business trip in South Carolina. I was lucky he was sitting beside me. He was going home to visit his parents. I am not a flyer. I am quite terrified of flying. Mike took my mind off the trip. Looking back, I fell in love with him on that 3-hour flight. His family has a history of flying. He was very proud of his wings. He told me flying was part of his DNA. His father and grandfather were both pilots in the great wars. I still remember how I chuckled when he told me his great grandfather led the air force in the civil war. At first I believed him. Mike was a very funny guy. "Was" is the word.

We got married and started a family. We have 3 kids. After 911, Mike lost his job due to downsizing and lack of seniority. Now our family is paying the price of what happened next.

When I first met Mike and when he was with the airline, he walked and talked with confidence. When this tall, dark, handsome man walked into the room his presence would almost stop all activity in the room. Everyone liked Mike.

After Mike was laid off, he tried to get another flying job. There were none. It took him a year to find another job. Not as a pilot but as a clerk pushing paper. He would come home crying to me and the kids. He went to a psychiatrist. He took sleeping pills at night and anti-depressants. Our bills were piling up. When Mike was flying for the airline he was making over $180,000 and we lived that lifestyle. I don't want to sound selfish, but it is very hard to go from living on a salary of $180,000 to $40,000. I am raising 2 kids and working too. It is tough. But what is tougher is seeing my husband's confidence evaporate. He is becoming a walking dead man. We always went out to parties. Now Mike won't leave the house. He says he is ashamed. He maintains he has broken the chain in his family. What prompted me to write this letter to you is the fact that last week Mike refused to go to his high school reunion. He says he never wants to see anyone who knew him from the past because they knew the person who he was not the person who he is today. I am wondering if I am the only person on the planet living this nightmare? Have others written to you with similar stories? Is their hope for Mike, the kids and myself?

You're Always Right – I'm Always Wrong

Dear Larry:

Elaine and I got married after going through horrible first marriages. We met on a blind date. I had never met anyone as smart as her. We would sit for hours and talk about world events. Unlike my first wife who did not graduate from high school, Elaine had her Ph.D. in English. Here I was a cab driver having a great time with someone so educated. She was my encyclopedia. I learned so much from our discussions. I really respected her intelligence. It was a turn on. She liked the fact I always liked to listen and learn from what she had to say. She said to me that I am the best listener she ever met. At the time I didn't find it offensive that she would correct my inaccurate comments. Now that we are married I can't stand the fact she thinks she is so smart. It is one thing to correct my grammar because that is what she studied. It is another thing when she criticizes my driving. Hey, I'm a taxi driver in New York City. She is telling me I don't know directions. I've been doing this for the last thirty years. I know this city like the back of my hand and I know how long it will take to get somewhere. I am beginning to feel that she looks down on me and I don't like it. It is a causing us to drift apart. I realize now that her teaching me during our courtship period was really her superiority complex in action. Does a college education make the person? How do I fix this mess without just driving off into the sunset?

Unfair Competition

Dear Larry:
I hate being compared to my brother-in-law. This guy is your typical Hollywood film industry guy. He thinks he's a big shot – three fancy cars, triple car garage, parties (which I attend), swimming pool, movie stars. You know the type — money no object people. My wife's sister met him on a cruise. I think I've heard the story 20 times about how they met. Quite honestly, I think she married him for the money and fun times, not because she loved him. I married my wife because I was in love. I know what love is. I live in Hollywood too. I run a gardening business. I can't compete with my brother-in-law yet my wife keeps asking "why can't we?" "Why don't we?" "What is wrong with us?" I was really hurt when her sister offered to pay for our trip to Australia to join them for a movie shoot. It hurts. I have pride. Unfortunately, my wife just can't accept me and our financial

situation. She constantly wants to be like her sister. This is starting to take a toll on not only our marriage but our bottom line. What do you do in a situation like this? My marriage is starting to fall apart. I just can't seem to get my wife to understand that we have each other. Why can't she understand that 'things' don't make a marriage wonderful?

Two For The Price of One

Dear Larry:

I heard about your website from an article in The Wall Street Journal. I love your website. I am writing you to warn people about the possible consequences of accepting gifts from parents and in-laws. When I first met my husband, Bill, he seemed very ambitious. He was running a printing business and had a used car business as well. The funny thing was he never seemed to have a dollar in his pocket. He would be asking his dad for a few bucks to make it through the week. His dad is generous, but very controlling. I didn't think anything of this when we were dating. I come from a family that just makes ends meet. My parents worked for other people all their lives. They never ran their own businesses. They always depended upon a salary. We were married about a year ago and things have not been pleasant. I feel that I married two men, not one. It all started when we got back from our honeymoon and we wanted to furnish the apartment. Bill and I went to the store to buy a chesterfield but we had a guest with us. His dad. I told my husband we should only buy what we could afford. He argued with me in front of the salesman that we could afford a better chesterfield (because he whispered to me – wink, wink, nudge, nudge, my dad is paying for it). I didn't like this, but I graciously accepted the gift. This tag along dad routine did not end at the furniture store. It kept repeating itself at every store we went to. I had to pick everything he wanted because his dad was paying for it. I don't want to sound unappreciative but when I got married I wanted one husband, not a boy and his father. I don't think my husband is ever going to grow up. He is an only child and just can't shake accepting handouts from his dad. He keeps telling me that his dad's money is going to be his money one-day any way. I hate this attitude. My husband is becoming lazy and all he does is take, take and take.

My House is Not Your Home

Dear Larry:

After being hammered in my divorce, it took me a while to get back on my feet financially. I have a good job. I bought a house, albeit smaller than the one I had to leave behind, but it is home. I've had my own home now for about a year and I am in a real predicament and I don't know what to do. I am in a serious relationship with a woman. I like her very much but there is a "but." She has 2 very young kids. She is a widow. I have two children but they are both in their early 20's. Our relationship has hit a critical juncture. She wants to move into my home with her two children. Up to now the relationship has been terrific. I see her everyday. But at the end of the day I go home to my house and she goes back to her apartment. Moving into my little castle from my point of view is out of bounds. She can't understand this. She says that we should be one happy family with all of us living under one roof. The problem is, we will not be one big happy family. There are too many issues that we can't resolve. One of the big issues is the children's behavior. She is a wonderful lady but a weak parent. She just can't say "no" to her kids. Up to this point, when I am at her apartment and the kids get unruly, I leave. What am I supposed to do in my house? I am not their parent. How will she look at me if I act as a disciplinarian? I have watched too many TV shows where the stepchild says: "you are not my father — you can't tell me what to do." Another issue is what if something happens to her? Who will raise the children? I know the answer and I don't like it. What if it doesn't work out? Will I lose part of my house or be thrown out? What about child support for her children? Would the court consider me their daddy? What about spousal support?

Praying For a Miracle

Dear Larry:

I met my husband on a retreat to Ireland. He was born in County Cork. I was born in Washington. He is Catholic and I am Protestant. My father is an Orangeman. My husband's parents are devout Catholics. They go to mass everyday. Growing up, my father always told me never to marry out of my faith. When I first met my husband, I did everything possible to avoid introducing him to the family. Between ourselves our religious differences were not important. They were important to our parents – my dad especially. I am realizing now that it was naïve for both of us to think that love would overcome the differences in our families. We are still very much in love. Unfortunately, my family refuses to see him and his family refuses to get together with my family and I. We feel like we are living on an island. We dread to think what will happen when we have our first child. Why can't people set aside their differences and let love prevail?

Screams At My Dreams

Dear Larry:

It is now 2am and I can't sleep. My mind is going back and forth trying to decide what to do. My wife has always been a conservative thinker. If she has a choice, she will always opt for the side that has little or no risk. Up to now, I admired this quality in her because she always invested our money safely and we still have our investments where many of our friends do not. The problem is that I want to give up my government job and go back to school to study law. I did well in college but I had to drop out because of family issues. My dream has always been to become a lawyer. I wrote the Law School Admission Test and did very well and I have been accepted at all the law schools I applied to. I surprised my wife with the news only to have my excitement destroyed when she screamed and said. "You are not going." What I thought was good news started a fight. I know that I can do well in law school and have heard that lawyer's in New York are starting at salaries of over $100,000 per year. I make half of that now. It will take me years in the government to reach that level of salary. It's not just the money. My happiness is at stake. I am not really happy with my job. I feel like a robot. My wife says stick with what you got because it is a job for life. I know that in a few years I will start to feel bitter because she made me miss this opportunity — an opportunity that doesn't come to everyone. Maybe I should not have gotten married until I was sure about my career.

The Three Rings of Marriage

I have had three bad marriages and I will never do it again (but I think I said that after the first one). There have also been 3 rings in those marriages — the engagement ring, the wedding ring and suffering.

Take a Walk and Have a Talk

Before you make any commitments, take a walk, have a talk and ask important questions. Get to know your future partner before you commit. Later it may be too late.

It's a Parent

Larry, as a parent I had to write you to help other parents out there. I urged my daughter to sign a pre-nuptial agreement before she got married. I even had her sit down with my attorney to get some advice. She wouldn't listen; She wouldn't listen to what I had to say about her future husband. She thought I was jealous about losing my little girl. Now we are both paying the price.

When my daughter was married, my wife and I gave them a home as a wedding gift. I also made my son-in-law a partner in the family business. About two years after their marriage my daughter visited us and told us that she was having marital problems. The next thing she knew her husband had hired an attorney and was claiming half the house and a piece of the family business. Well, that day marked the beginning of the war between them and between my wife and I and our ex-son-in-law. The house ended up being sold. My business suffered. I eventually had to pay a lot of money to buy my son-in-law out of the business that I had started and worked night and day to build up. Now my daughter lives with us and with her son. Parents—even if your kids tell you to bud out, don't listen. If they won't sign a pre-nup, then don't ever give them money!

Teen Bride

Am I missing something here? When my mom got married in the 1950's she was 19. That was not an uncommon age to get married. My daughter is 19 and wants to get married ASAP. I cannot convince her that getting married at 19 then is not the same as getting married at 19 now. How do you convince her that she is probably making a mistake when she argues that her grandmother was married for over 50 years? She thinks that just because her grandmothers' marriage lasted so long that everything was perfect just like it is in the movies.

Nothing In Common Law

Thank goodness I didn't give in. He was so anxious to get married and I said no let's live together to get to know each other better. He said he didn't want to live in sin, I said it would be a bigger sin if we got divorced. We dated for about six months and thought we really knew each other. We really didn't get to know one another until we had to share the same tube of toothpaste. Are we ever different? When you really love someone and are compatible it doesn't matter if he squeezes the tube in the middle. But when it just isn't working even the smallest idiosyncrasy can create tension. As you can probably tell we are not together. The price? Well, no lawyers, no court appearances only some emotional scarring. Hey, I'll get over it and move on. It could have been a lot worse.

I Survived a War and a Divorce

My wife (ex-wife) and I met in Saigon. I was wrapping up my tour of duty and she was a nurse from a well-placed Vietnamese family. I thought that I had found the princess of Saigon. She was beautiful, gentle and genuine. Boy, I don't know whether it was the American air or water or food, but did she change when she made it state side. I will never forget the first time I laid eyes on her. She was a spot of paradise in the middle of a cesspool. It is sad that I look back at those horrible days with nostalgia because of what I am going through today. I've lost everything, including my personal dignity. Lawyer's letters, threats, false accusations I frankly can't take it anymore. I never understood how bad divorce could be until I lived through it myself. She's even poisoned my kid's minds against me. I feel all alone. I just had to write you because no one else wants to listen and this is my way of dealing with it.

My In-Law Is An Outlaw

I am so embarrassed because of my father-in-laws reputation. What kind of reputation does he have? Well, he's known as a swindler, a liar, a thief and a cheat. I never knew this until my wife convinced me to move from Dallas to her father's small town, which I will keep confidential. Once I began working for my father-in-law I began to hear whispers at the bank, at the gas station, in the barbershop, all around town about him. I am a Chartered Accountant and my father-in-law is the only financial planner for 100 miles. It was really a perfect fit. At least I thought so until I heard the rumors. As time went on and I began to become a fixture around the place, many of the residents questioned how I could have ever become part of that family. I didn't know what they were talking about. One day I was even threatened by a big bruiser who told me that my father-in-law had lost his mother's life savings. I can't make a friend. I can't go to the movies. I can't even go to the gym. Who says you don't marry your in-laws as well as your spouse?

The Boss – spelled backwards is double s. o. b.

My husband of 12 years was the sweetest, warmest guy you could ever have imagined. We went on trips, took walks in the park, went to movies at least once a week and he was very romantic and loving. Then he got a promotion to become a manager at the bank. I never see him. When he comes home, I don't know who he is. He is short with me. He just wants to eat and be left alone. We even are starting to sleep in separate rooms. He makes it a habit of crashing out in front of the TV every night. He is not interested in making love. He keeps saying, if you are not happy, go see a lawyer. I don't know if he is joking or he is serious. But one day I might just take him up on his offer. Isn't marriage supposed to be mutually satisfying? In speaking with my friends, many of their husbands are also taking their marriage for granted. Is this becoming a trend?

Tarzan and Cheater

If you think cheating is fun and exciting, listen to what happened to me. After 25 years, my marriage was becoming run of the mill and boring – no passion, no romance, nothing.

Friends of mine were telling me they were having affairs too, as they say, "add some spice to their life." One even told me his girl-friend's friend was looking for some excitement in her life as well. He hooked us up. I felt guilty and awkward at first, but it was fun, and lets face it, you only have one life. The operative word is fun. It's very strange because you never seem to think you will create emotional fireworks with the person you are cheating with. My cheating part-ner was married to a trucker. He was only home 2 days every two weeks. Hey, I was doing her a favor. She was lonely and sexually unsatisfied. When we began, we both agreed that it would be just for now and not for the future. I never wanted to get involved with any-one else. I am married and so is she. I have kids. I have a career. I know this sounds like I am two faced, but a deal is a deal. She didn't see it that way. Last week the fun stopped when she told me that she wanted me to leave my wife and eventually marry her. I told her it was out of the question. She told me that if I didn't go along with her plan she was going to call my wife, my boss and tell her husband, who she said would break both my legs if he found out. I told her it is over and now I am living in fear.

Dating Burn Out

Everyone keeps telling me how wonderful it is to be in the dating stage of relationships. Yuk. Yuk. I am sick and tired of telling the same stories about myself to different women every week. I am jealous of my friends who are married and have moved on with their lives. At first I was very arrogant. No one was good enough for me. This one had a big nose. This one wasn't as thin as I'd like. This one liked jazz and not rock. You know what I mean. I'm almost ready to settle for the next number that comes up on the roulette wheel. My advice to people out there — don't be so picky. No one is perfect. It took me a long time to realize this.

A Good Son Makes for a Good Husband

All you women out there who are complaining that your husbands are too close to their mothers should read this. I am a two-timed divorced woman and I regret the first divorce more than you can imagine. It took something really bad to happen to realize that I had something good but threw it away. It really bothered me that, Bill, my first husband, wouldn't put me ahead of his mother. He always told me we were equal. He loved us both equally, but in different ways. I must admit that he was very good to me — never forgot a birthday or anniversary, breakfast in bed on Mother's Day — I'm sure you get the idea. But, there was always his mother. He would run to her whenever she called. He once told me he read somewhere that a good son makes for a good husband. Ya, I laughed at him and said you have to make a choice — if there were two hands sticking out of the water and you had to choose, which one would you pull out? His answer was always that I would pull out both. I always said that was impossible. You married me, not your mother. This devotion to his mother really got to me when he canceled our Christmas vacation because his mother was not feeling well. His response was it was his obligation to look after his mother in her old age since she had always been there for him when he was a child. But don't get me wrong. He was a great husband, but I could not take the competition anymore. That canceled trip did it. I told him to take his mother and have a nice day. I went to a lawyer and got divorced. I vowed that the next man I hooked up with would love only me and no one else. I met Charlie at a bar in Lexington. He was newly divorced. He was the rugged type. No mommas boy here. As a matter of fact I pictured him with a Stetson riding his horse across the west. Charlie was very proud of the fact he was a self made man. He rarely bothered with his family and had no kids of his own. He always maintained that Mother's Day and Father's Day were a waste of time and just a way of helping the department stores and florists make some money. We dated for about a year and got married. His independence and rugged nature were a real turn on for me. After we got married, I began to see a Charlie I didn't like. Looking back, I don't think Charlie changed, but I believe that I just ignored this side of him. He had no respect for woman. His favorite saying was, "all you broads are the same." He didn't do the little things that my first husband did that I now realize were very important — no flowers, no kind words, no interest in my career — it was all about Charlie. Needless to say, our marriage lasted 8 months. Last month I had to eat crow. Bill's mom, past away. Out of respect I went to the funeral. I saw Bill and his new wife walking hand in hand. And I saw the love he was showing to his new wife and I broke down in tears because of what I foolishly and selfishly gave up.

The Horror Scope

I am a Sagittarius and he is a Virgo. Who cares? He does. When we first met it gave us something to talk about. The horoscope god said that we were compatible. It was a harmless and fun interest until about a year into our marriage. I remember the day like it was yesterday because I call it my horror scope day. On the way to work we stopped off to have a coffee and we read our daily horoscope. His said that he should not be operating machinery that day. To me it was all hocus-pocus and at that moment we both brushed it off as nothing. Well, as we pulled out of the parking lot of the coffee shop, smack- we had our first automobile accident. Ever since that day, Mr. Virgo lives and breathes by his horoscope. At last count, he had just been fired from his fourth job because on his off days, he refuses to go to work. It got so bad, that he would not have sex with me unless he consulted his moon chart and confirmed that all his planets were in alignment. This stuff was too much and it was getting on my nerves. We had a lot of fights about this. Mr. Virgo was turning into Mr. Psycho. I was really getting to the breaking point. Something had to give. I love him, but minus the addiction. So one day I decided to take his book and write in it, 'your horoscope for today is, if you don't change you are going to get divorced.' It worked.

Wait a Second

Larry, I am in a quandary. I have 3 teenagers. I lost my wife in a car accident 4 years ago. What's it really like to live in what people often refer to as a "blended family?" On TV it looks so easy. Everyone seems so happy. The reason I am posing this question is because I am dating a woman with two of her own teenage sons. I know eventually I am going to have to make a decision — marry her with the kids or end it. I hate to sound mean, but I cannot ever see myself living under one roof with her kids. How can I not favor my kids over hers? How can I hug her kids in front of my kids? Isn't this going to create jealousy? What about money? Isn't it natural for a parent to want the best for his/her children? Well what happens if you can only afford it for your own kids and not for hers? Is this not going to create problems? My girlfriend thinks I worry too much. She says it will all work out. Thousands of second married couples do it. I would really appreciate hearing from some couples who have made navigating (successful or not) through these waters of second relationship romance.

Pulling Out My Heir

Dear Larry:

I never realized how complicated and unnerving a second marriage could be until we went to our lawyer's office to make a new will. My last will was made when my first wife and I got married. It was easy, she got what was mine, and I got what was hers and then it went to the kids. The appointment took half an hour and was surprisingly pleasant. I never dreamed that my next will appointment would be one of the worst experiences of my life. The fact is, the will appointment with my second wife almost caused us to break up. Looking back on the experience, it was because I did not have your book and did not consider some very important issues. Here is what happened.

I have two kids from my first marriage and my wife has three kids from her marriage. We have no children together. My kids are older now and my wife's kids are still in their early teens. We both came to the marriage with assets. I have substantially more assets than she does. My intention, when I walked into the lawyer's office, was to have my eldest son be the executor of my will and that I would leave a small portion of my estate to my wife and the majority to my kids. I did not feel I should leave anything to her kids when I passed away because I am taking care of them now, while I am alive. I assumed she would take care of her kids in her will. The big mistake I made was not discussing this with her before we arrived at the lawyer's office and before we got married. When our lawyer asked us what we wanted in our wills I told her my intentions and my wife told her that she expected me to leave everything to her in my will and she would leave everything to me in her will and that when we both passed away, everything would be divided equally amongst the 5 kids.

I could not agree with her thinking. I had some major concerns and voiced them at the meeting. My biggest concern was that my wife might change her will after I die and cut my kids out of her will altogether. I brought a lot of money into this marriage. I have a business and I inherited two hotels from my father. I feel my kids should get the bulk of what is left of my estate when I die. Needless to say my reasoning did not go over well with my wife. She accused me of not trusting her. As I said earlier, my intention was to have my eldest son be the executor of my estate. She did not buy that. She wanted to be a co-executor with my son so she could work with my son in that role. Isn't there some kind of conflict that can arise here? We spent a great deal of time in the lawyer's office fighting over this issue. She could not understand my feelings. She brought very little in the way of assets into the marriage and yet she thinks her kids are entitled to an equal part of my estate. I inherited a cottage from my dad. My brother and I promised my dad we would keep it in the family. She wants me to leave my share of the cottage to her. I want to leave it to my brother because he is leaving his share to me. To top it all off, one of my wife's kids is going to require a lot of money for care because of a learning disability. I've told my wife that during my lifetime I will do my best to help that child, but after I die, I don't think it is fair that my kids don't get a bigger share of my estate. In front of the lawyer, my wife cried, yelled, called me names (cheap, selfish, etc.) and then went into her silent mode. I've never felt so embarrassed and distant from her. She feels what's mine belongs to her and what's hers belongs to her children in equal portions with my kids. It didn't stop there. The lawyer then brought up another good point –what if we get sick or have an accident and become incapacitated? I want my eldest son to be my power of attorney. He knows my finances intimately. He works beside me every day and I want him to have the power to sign for me if I am out to lunch. My wife was very upset that I would not want her to make those choices. She says I don't trust her. I've known my son for over 30 years and I've known my wife for only a few years. Sure I trust her, but what if she gets involved with someone else if I get sick? Will she act in my best interests? I am concerned that if she has access to my large estate she may squander my money. I told the attorney this and she suggested that both my wife and my son could be my powers of attorney. This arrangement would at least provide a check and balance. My wife refused. She wanted to be the only one. It's as if my marriage license gives her a license over everything I worked for. Needless to say, we got nothing accomplished in that 2-hour session except to realize that we did not have as much in common as we thought we did. Someone once told me that money can get in the way of love. It sure looks that way. I love my wife and I love my children from my first marriage but I am not willing to risk my children's future. I like what you (Larry) have to say about second time arounders in your book. I now realize that section in your book should be mandatory reading for anyone thinking of getting married for a second time. I wish both of us had done so. It is a real eye opener.

Fun, Fun, Fun – At a price!

Why is it that everyone talks about cheating but no one talks about the voices you hear in your head after the fun has gone?

I was married for about 12 years. I was your average American spouse – house, kids, dog even a white picket fence. What was missing from my life was some fun. My separated girlfriends kept saying that they were having fun, fun, fun. I had to admit that I was a little envious. Here I was cooking dinner for my husband while my girlfriends were being wined, dined and romanced by their boyfriends. One day, a few weeks ago, my husband went away on a business trip. My kids were staying over at their friend's house. My girlfriends thought this would be a great time to get together. They believed I needed to have some fun. I agreed. I thought it would just be a night out with the girls. We all met at this restaurant. When I got there all the girls had their dates. They even had one for me. At first I was really angry and very uncomfortable. But this fellow they set me up with was very hot. Yes, I was angry, but as the night went on and because I had just turned 40, he and I were in the right place at the right time. You might say, our stars had aligned. After dinner, we all met up at one of the girl's condos. When we arrived, we all decided to watch a DVD. In front of my eyes, this condo became a steamy drive in movie. Everyone was making out and before I knew it, so was I. The next morning I couldn't live with myself. I couldn't look at myself in the mirror. The guilt was overwhelming. All day long as I did the household chores, I kept thinking about what I had done and about my husband. Every time someone looked at me or spoke to me, I thought they knew. Had my girlfriends said anything? To this day, Larry, I have not told my husband about what happened but I am terrified that he and my children will find out. I am even afraid that I might talk about it in my sleep. That few minutes of fun has turned into a perpetual feeling of guilt that just won't go away. What have I done?

Preying Mantis

Larry, not only did I lose my kids, but they lost their daddy and their heritage. I was married in 1994. My wife was Catholic and I am Jewish. When I first met my wife, my parents were not pleased that I was marrying outside of my faith. My wife's family was indifferent. I am not a religious person, but heritage is important to me. My wife agreed to convert and she convinced me it was not just a symbolic conversion done for my family's acceptance but because she wanted it and wanted our children to be Jewish by birth. Eight years later, my wife left me and got custody of our two children. I see the kids, now 5 and 8, every second weekend and once during the week. A few weeks ago, I picked the kids up like I normally do and in their knapsack were books about Christianity. When I asked my 8 year old where he got the book he told me he got it from the church library. I was shocked. He also told me he wanted a certain item for Christmas. I called my wife and asked what was going on. She told me that she had a religious re-conversion. She told me she never really wanted to convert to Judaism. She had converted just to appease my parents and me. Her intent now was to show our children the religion she grew up with. After I heard this I was sick.

Free Speech

When I read your opening chapter about speeches at weddings I just had to write you. I am divorced and just recently came across my wedding video. I don't know what possessed me to watch it, but I did. I can't believe what a farce that day was. My wife and my in-laws put on a great act that day. They deserve an award for acting It killed me to watch my father-in-law with those fake tears rolling down his cheeks saying how happy he was to have my family and me as part of his family. Sure that was then, the day after the wedding he called my parents and told them they were cheap for not having more money for expensive flowers. My father is a laborer. To him a dollar is a dollar. And how my father-in-law told everyone he now had a son and that I was now part of the family. How does this explain an affidavit he swore accusing me of being "a monster?" And my wife even made a speech telling everyone the wedding day was the happiest moment of her life. How does that explain an email she sent me telling me that she had been unhappy from the moment we left the church till now? What a crock. I believe in freedom of speech but I believe everyone should take an oath before they speak at a wedding.

Thank you, thank you, thank you

Larry I had to email you after I heard you on the radio yesterday. You know you are right that separation and divorce is a horrible experience. But sometimes the person that thinks they are going to be the winner ends up finishing last and the person who they thought would finish last comes out of nowhere to win. According to my ex, I was the worst person you could ever have imagined. Who the heck would ever want me? I was just so lucky that she overlooked all of my faults and hot buttons and married me. She was the gift of all gifts to mankind — smart-ambitious-precious. That is, according to her and her family. Well, Larry, she is on boyfriend number 5 and I am with fiancé number one. We plan to be married in the next few months. She is a great lady. Loves me for who I am. When I tell her what my ex said about me, she wonders how I could have endured that mental abuse for so long. We all have our faults. No one is perfect, but some people can't accept people for who they are but are intent on changing them. Sometimes things work out for the best.

I Do Believe

Larry the conclusion of your book touched me. I have been married to my wonderful husband for over 60 years. We were best friends when we married and still are. I don't know how we are going to live without each other someday, but that day is, regrettably, fast approaching. My husband is very ill, and sadly, because of his illness, does not know who I am. I don't want to leave you with the impression that our marriage was always smooth sailing. It wasn't. But we weathered the storms by always reminding ourselves, and each other, that we are the best of friends. If one of us forgot, we would quickly remind the other. Whenever we had a tiff (most times it was over nothing) neither of us ran out, slammed the door and drove away to cool down. That only makes things worse and creates terrible memories that are hard to erase. We always did little things for each other. My husband often bought me little gifts of thanks. I never wanted expensive gifts — neither did he. To us, the thought was always more important than the gift. And the cards he made for me were always hand made. Not because he could not afford a store bought card, but because he wanted to take the time and make the card for me. Larry, how many people keep the cards they receive? I have kept every one because they mean so much to me knowing they were made from the heart. My husband worked in a factory. He never got praise. He often came home full of stress. I always made a point of thanking him for his hard work and for providing for our family. I also never put any excess stress on him. So many of my friends were never satisfied with what they had. They always wanted more and were willing to put stress on each other and the family to get there. Many of them would go into debt in order to buy a bigger house or go on trips. We were always satisfied with what we had and would never buy anything unless we could afford it. We always made do with what we had. It troubles me when I see so many marriages failing today. It is hard to believe that all of those broken marriages had problems that could not have been worked out. I don't want to sound like a philosopher, but maybe people should look the other way. Maybe they should "bite their tongue" before they say something that will hurt. And maybe they should realize the person they are marrying is not a mirror image of themselves — they are different unique people. Best friends, thank-you's and respect. Those are the ingredients that made our marriage last.

A Course For Divorce

In my opinion there should be a course on relationships. I don't think it is enough to just teach kids about the facts of life and birth control. The fact is there are too many divorces out there. As you state in your book you cannot fly an airplane without having taken the course. Why then do we allow people to marry and have children without any training? I am a statistician. I like to look at the effects things have on other things. Without sounding too much like a professor, let's look at some of the ramifications this lax attitude towards marriage and divorce have on society. Currently, there is a 50% divorce rate. Other than lawyers, actuaries, real estate agents, etc. benefiting from this fractured family phenomenon, there are more subtle fallouts. What appears to the naked eye to be a short-term interruption in the life of the "family" has a long-term intergenerational effect.

In my opinion, the facts speak for themselves. You have a couple that once lived together now having to live separate and apart. Not only does this leave emotional scares, but from an economical point of view, it weakens the financial foundation for the next generation.

In fact, that next generation may have to look to government funding for help. Let me explain. With the assumption that parents want the best for their children and assuming, of course, the parents want better for their children than they had for themselves, parents have a common goal of bettering the family. From a financial perspective, the family nest egg is used to provide for the children's well being — their maintenance and education. When the family unit is divided, the egg cracks and rarely returns to the egg it once was. Let me explain. When a divorce occurs, the husband hires a lawyer and the wife hires a lawyer. Generally, it is the husband that is forced to vacate the home and requires somewhere new to live. He either has to purchase a home or rent. With this, the husband is required to spend money on new furnishings, appliances, insurance, an automobile, etc. Great for the economy but tragic for the once treasured nest egg. What this "fracturing" does is double the expenses and halves the long term financial benefits for the children. You now have children who were once set up for a fully paid college education now being forced to scramble for government grants, scholarships or student loans. Some of my research has shown that some of these children end up in low paying jobs and never go on to higher levels of education. The bottom line is, even though the parents want to, they just don't have enough money to fund a college education. I shudder to think of the emotional impact this has upon a child who once had dreams of a college degree. I can go on and on. I hope I have made my point. Maybe what I have said will have an impact on some of those people who believe that divorce is not a big deal. In my opinion, it is.

A Desperate Cry

After seeing you on television and listening to the calls, I just had to email you. People like my 16-year-old brother and I are the silent victims of divorce. We are silent victims, because we really had little choice when our parents divorced. They (our parents) treated us like we were pieces in a game. My mom and my dad, who we once called mommy and daddy, were trying to show a judge that it was in our best interests to live with them. Does anyone really understand what it is like to hear parents who once tucked us in together at night become so mean towards each other and yet on the other hand be so nice to us as if nothing bad is going on in our lives? We know what is going on. My parents acted as if this was something that just happened and that we should carry on as if nothing had changed. Well life did change when my parents split. Every second weekend my brother and I would travel to my dad's house. He waited for us outside. He was mostly on time. When he was not on time my mother was very angry because she had things to do and we always felt we were just in the way during her free time. Dad never came to the door. My mother looked at him as if he was a taxi driver. We got into the car and drove away for our weekend with dad. All weekend, dad acted like he was a counselor at camp. We had lots of fun. Dad never disciplined us. He was more of a friend than a dad. I missed having a father figure in my life. My best friend and his dad, who was not from a divorced family, would do things together that my dad would never do. Our weekends were always filled with activities — swimming, baseball, amusement parks and more. We never cut the grass together, we never went to the home improvement store together, we never bought a new tool together, and we never built a deck together. It was as if dad thought the way to our hearts was by having fun. I don't know why dad felt that when mom and him broke up — he had to stop being a regular dad. When he would drop us off at mom's house at the end of our visit, it would take my brother and I a while to get back to the routine that mom had set up for us. Who felt like picking up the dishes after eating in restaurants all weekend? Who felt like helping with the laundry and other household chores? It was a constant battle of two different lifestyles. I couldn't wait to get out and live on my own, which I now do. The problem is my brother. He still lives with my mother and he has to for 2 more years. Lately, he has been telling me he believes that he is the cause of the divorce. I am concerned about his future. He tells me he will never get married because he never wants to put his kids through what we experienced. He tells me he wants to quit school. He seems to have lost his youthful innocence. What is really troubling him now is that mom is getting married to her boyfriend who has 3 of his own teenage sons. My brother keeps telling me how he is going to be trampled on by his new brothers. He is not happy.

I wrote this to you because I want everyone who reads this to understand that children of divorce do suffer and often suffer in silence. What are otherwise happy days for other children can be tragic days for children of divorced parents. Imagine what it is like to open gifts on Christmas morning without your father being there to share in your joy. What it is like to celebrate your birthday twice — once with your father and his side of the family and again with your mother and her side of the family. Or what it is like to tell your teacher you need two separate times for parents night at school because your parents won't be in the same room together. Or be in a school play when your parents are sitting at opposite ends of the auditorium. I dread what is going to happen on my wedding day when my parents are going to have to face all my relatives and friends.

Father's Day

People think dad's who don't have custody of their children don't want their kids and are happy to have the freedom to do what they want in life. Let me set the record straight for all of you who think this way – I lost my children to my wife who cheated on me. I did nothing to deserve losing custody of three of the people I lived for. My three kids mean everything to me and yet some judge had the power to decide that they would be better off with their mother. What can my kids be thinking about me? I don't want to be honest and tell them the reason we split up was because their mother cheated on me. And how do I explain to them that some judge decided that it is not in their best interests to be with me? I am not the only one in this situation. There are many other fathers like me who dearly love their kids but the law only entitles them to see the kids periodically and say goodnight by phone during the week.

I belong to a group of dad's who only have access to their children, not custody. They all tell me how much they love their children. It's not fair and quite frankly, it is a tragedy. Tragic for us, but more so for the kids.

From One to Another

Hey Larry:

Glad to see that you talked about more than just the personal side of relationships in your book. It is important you touched on the financial and legal aspects. I am a relationship writer for a local paper and I am always telling my editors they should get someone to write about the legal and monetary impact of marriage and divorce. Bravo!

A Lawyer Looks Back

I really enjoyed your book. What impressed me most was your section on separation and divorce and your words of wisdom regarding amicable separations. I am a family law attorney. I was known as the lawyer you went to when you wanted to win at all costs. I was tuff and non-emotional. The opposing side was nothing more than a file folder. It was not a person. It had no feelings. It was in my eyes "the enemy." My practice thrived and I got a thrill every time I won a case for my client or when I played the game right and the opposing side fell for my poker face tactics. My goal with every case was to get the best possible result for my client. The word "amicable" when it came to separation was not in my vocabulary. But that all changed one day when a young woman came into my office. She looked like a teenager, but she was in her early 20s. Too young I thought to have been married and seeking a divorce. My initial hunch was right because she wasn't there to talk about herself but had come to tell me what I had done to her family. As it turned out, her mother was a former client of mine. I remember having fought a vicious battle with her father's lawyer over custody of this young woman who was then 10 years old. I remember this case specifically because the mother was ready to give in to her father's pleas and agree to shared custody. But I told the mother she should be seeking sole custody because it would be easier for her to deal with visitation, vacations, teachers, etc.. With sole custody, everything would be on her terms. With sole custody of her daughter, she was in the driver's seat and could include her ex-husband whenever she felt it was appropriate. I remember vividly the husband would not accept this and fought our plan every step of the way. When it was all said and done, the court held in our favor and we won the case. My client was very pleased with the results and I felt a feeling of victory that is difficult to describe. I didn't realize the impact of that victory until I met with that child in my office that day. In fact, that day was a turning point for me. It had been almost ten years since that day in court. Her first words, that day, to me were that I had destroyed her family. She told me how the decision of the judge and my brilliant legal tactics had devastated her father. I could see how angry and hurt she was. She told me how her father played that day over and over in his mind and in conversations with her. "He was never the same," she said. She told me how she slowly saw her father change from being a daddy, to a dad, to an uncle, to a friend and then finally to an acquaintance. She told me how her father depleted most of his life savings to fight for her. She noted that he not only lost most of his money but, most importantly, his dignity because he ended up living in his parent's basement. She told me she was still mourning the death of her father who passed away from a heart attack a few weeks ago and how my name had come up at the funeral as being a contributing cause of his death. I told her I was fighting for her best interests. She told me her best interests would have been to have involvement from both her mother and her father as parents with equal rights. After she left my office, I heard her words ringing in my head for days. I didn't sleep for weeks after that. I kept thinking about how many other young kids and their parents I had affected. I realize now winning does not necessarily have to mean there is a winner and a loser. Winning can also mean compromise where everyone wins. From that day forward, I applied this to my practice. It is for this reason I recommend people send a copy of your book to anyone they know who is or is thinking about separating.

Divorce Brings On The Dislocation Blues

Hi Larry:

It was great to read the article in the paper about your opinion on separation and divorce. Having been recently divorced myself, I would now strongly discourage anyone from walking down this path if they can possibly avoid it. It is devastating to the individuals involved (no one wins!) and absolutely horrible for children. I call children the "silent victims".

In my situation, my husband is with a major drug company. We moved to our present location — San Francisco ten years ago however, both my former husband and myself are from New York. To make a long story short, infidelity on my husband's part was the cause of the divorce. We have three children. Here I am — across the continent from my family, brought here by my husband's career, now trying to struggle on and make some sort of a stable life for myself and my children. As I am driving around in my car in this city, I often look around and wonder "what the heck am I doing here?" My kids are now older and have developed roots here. It would be very hard now to pick up and go back to New York. It is a very lonely feeling. We came here as a family with such high expectations of a good life together. The brokenness that divorce creates is phenomenal.

Let's pass the word — DIVORCE HURTS! Lets put a stop to this debilitating human condition.

Bad News Boyfriend Sows Seeds That Yield
a Harvest of Discontent

Larry:

We have a 21-year-old daughter who we think is making the biggest mistake of her life. I hope she will read your book and maybe it will help. I'm going to order it today. We now hardly see her because of the relationship she has with someone we cannot stand. We have tried to talk to her but, of course, she won't listen. They think they are going to get married and live happily ever after. She has told me I am crazy, making things up about "Mr. Wonderful" and I have no credibility. She once valued our opinions, but not anymore. Isn't it amazing how someone so naïve doesn't think they have anything at all to learn from someone that has been married for 23 years? The boyfriend has convinced her that I (her mom) am a bad influence, etc. She is being so manipulated she doesn't even act like herself anymore. There are so many warning signs we see with this guy but she chooses not to. I wish she would open her eyes. Anything that is wrong in the relationship either gets blamed on us or she takes the blame herself. He comes from an abusive family. He is controlling, manipulative and jealous. Don't we have every right to be concerned? I think the problems would become 100 times worse if they were to get married. We feel like we have lost our daughter, maybe forever. She has gone from writing me letters telling me what a great mom I was to sending emails telling me how awful her life was when she lived at home and how terrible I am. It is pretty hard to deal with. I will never have respect for her boyfriend because he has messed with her head and convinced her we are evil, horrible people.

I hope that book gets here FAST!

Engagement Warning Not Heeded – "I Should Have Seen It Coming – Now I am Miserable"

I am a married, 29 year old, woman. We have been together for 6 years, married for 4 years, (and) I don't know what to think. My husband (31 years old) has an alcohol problem, which I knew about when we were engaged. We have had some trying times, bills not being paid and creditors calling all the time. Then I snapped and made him choose me or the bottle. He went to an addiction center. He had convinced them and himself that he could beat it.

One day he was stressed out from work, he was drinking and driving and had a wreck with the car. That night he lost his license for 1 year. He told me he wouldn't drink anymore, and pleaded for me to stand by him through this trying time. He did good for 6 H months, then he started to drink again because "he can control how much he drinks." Now we are at the same place we were 1 year ago. I just so badly want the sober husband that I love and care for. He is such a different person when he drinks. He has a buddy he does everything with (drinking, hunting, and fishing every chance they get) and sometimes I feel this friend of his should be wearing my wedding band. I am finding it harder to talk without blowing up. For the last 3 nights I have been in the spare bedroom. The thought of anything sexual between us when he drinks disgusts me.

I know it sounds like I am making it out to be all his fault. He doesn't go out to bars; he hasn't cheated on me (I know). I start a lot of the arguments, by saying, "we could of bought that if you didn't drink all the money away" or "why not have another beer allkie," and I know that this is hurtful to him, but I'm hurting too.

This past week I have been planning to leave but can't. I want us to be happy. I am at my wits ends and don't know what to do.

I know as long as our problems are here, I will never bring a child into this troubled marriage. And that is very sad for me to say.

I do want your book. Maybe it will help me see a light at the end of my tunnel. I hope I can get him to read it.

Cure For Divorce? – The laws must be changed!

Dear Larry:

My son's story sheds light on why divorce is so popular today. It is the law. My son was married for 12 years. He has 2 daughters ages 6 and 9. They had it all — healthy kids, their health, no mortgage, great careers and money in the bank. After the house was paid for, my ex-daughter-in-law told him she wanted a divorce. She had met someone else. He was forced to leave. The law says the kids automatically stay with the mother (provided she is fit). He now has to pay over half of his salary for child support. More importantly, the kids are now without a full time father. If the law stated the kids automatically stay half the time with dad and half the time with mom, there would be no child support. The law is clear — when a woman gets tired of her husband she just has to hire a lawyer, throw her husband out and reap the benefits of ridiculously large amounts of child support (do 2 children really require $1200 dollars and expense money every month to survive if the mother is working and bringing in a six figure income?). If the laws were re-written so that in the event of divorce, the kids spent half the time with the mother and half the time with the father (provided both are fit to care for the kids) the divorce rate would decrease dramatically. If families are to remain intact the laws must be changed.

In Separation "Hell" There is No Justice

Here is a case that is very close to our family and may be of interest to you. I am writing to you as a very concerned spouse, parent, and cousin / friend of someone going through a divorce process now. Let me elaborate on how my cousin's situation has come about and where it seems to be heading at this point in time.

Like yourself, he too was in a happy marriage, which started at a young age — he was 21, she was 19. Married for almost 20 years with three beautiful boys now ages 6, 13 and 16. Over two years ago he discovered his ex-wife was having an extra-marital affair after much denial on her part. He sought out counseling but she put up much resistance to it and simply stated she no longer wanted to be with him. She continued her active social life with her new lover even while he stood by the kids, continued his work and tried to sort out where to go from there.

It's been almost a year and a half since he moved out of his own house at her insistence. She had ways of making life uncomfortable for him. He had no place else to go but his parent's home. In the process of all this his mother was dying of cancer to which his wife showed no compassion to him. In fact, she made things even more unbearable and difficult.

He has the children one weekend every two weeks and sees them, that is, takes care of them, when she goes on a galavanting expedition. She often uses them as a threatening mechanism toward him to get more money from him. She works only part-time at a doctor's office.

His financial situation is worsening. He is paying her over $2000 per month in child support and extras. He only clears $3000 per month. She is still living in their home while he lives in his parent's basement!

This may sound very one sided, but this is it. How can we help? I fear for his deteriorated health. He wants to get on with his life, get the 50% share of the house, the property, he owns and move on. She wants her cake and eat it too! This is totally unfair, unjust and morally inhuman to have an individual live like this, to be stuck in this state without any legal justice.

Con Man Sets New Wife Up For Life.....
Of Debt and Misery

To all single women and men who own assets, please, please before going into a marriage or a live in situation, read my story!

I was a single parent for 15 years, raised my 2 daughters myself, had my own business and my house was paid for. Life was good.

Had two long-term relationships with great men that were well respected in the community and both were successful businessmen. Both came with offers of marriage (I had known these men for years prior to dating them.) However, with my independence, I opted to stay single.

Suddenly, without warning I met a man who could not do enough for me, catered to me, and was very, very generous. We traveled the entire year we dated.

Marriage came quickly. He talked me into selling my house and into buying another one.

Suddenly, one week after marriage, this man turned into a monster. We were separated 4 times in the first year.

He begged to come back and promised to make a successful go of it.

Turns out he was a con man and hadn't finished setting me up!

He had so much debt he hid from me. He ended up having $92,000 worth of liens on the house without my knowledge. The house was sold during the divorce and all his debt was satisfied from my proceeds! (We never filed joint taxes).

He came into marriage with nothing and went out with everything. Now I am broke and have no home.

I want to give your readers a few pre-marriage hints:

1. Protect your assets ...if they give you a hard time, bail out!
2. Look for stability in financial situations.
3. Do they have credit cards? Do they throw money around?
4. Do they show respect for you, your friends and family?
5. Are they in a hurry to get married or live together? RED

FLAG!

6. Do they have close relationships with friends and their family? If not, why?

7. If your friends tell you they do not approve of the relationship...chances are you better really give it a lot of thought!

Hope your readers really pay attention to details! Your book is a long time coming!!!

Looking To The Future

Dear Larry:

I decided to change my radio program at work the other day and listened to your program, and I was amazed at what you had to say. It seemed to have come at the right time.

I have been through TWO marriages. So too has the person I am currently dating. We are both in our early 50's and have been dating for about a year and a half. Of course, we are both hesitant about making any major commitments and are still in the romantic, can't get enough of each other stage. I have been thinking about what the future will bring for us as a couple and therefore I am seeing things about him lately that never showed up before. I am very anxious to get your book and hopefully become enlightened by other people's experiences. Great idea you have and good luck.

Don't Throw In The Towel

Dear Larry:

Once again an interesting topic. Just a personal comment on the institution of marriage.

I'm 25 and have been married 5 years. My wife and I have been through trials, the death of a child and feelings of distance between us at times. All situations where it would have been easier to just walk away. But we didn't.

It seems a great deal of people feel it is better to throw in the towel rather than try and work at it. I think people of my generation believe if it doesn't work out (anything in life) they have wasted their time. It touches on the whole issue of yesterday's phone in as well. So many people are not willing to sacrifice in order to go the distance.

My wife and I are committed to keeping the communication between us flowing and are always willing to listen to each other.

Those are my thoughts. Thanks

It Takes Two

Dear Larry:

I heard you on a local radio station and thought I would investigate your website. I have read the stories posted. All of the stories tore at my heart. To date, I have been married for 11 years (first marriage). I am going to share with you my story.... without placing blame entirely on my spouse.

I'd like to describe my husband. He loves the children with all his heart and therefore is a great dad. He is dedicated to his job and also loves what he is doing. Our relationship.... Well, it's like we are just two people sharing a house. We don't have any "major" disagreements. However, we don't "communicate" our needs. This "communication" issue was brought up in the first year of marriage. We decided we should seek counseling and we went two times...the problem hasn't gone away. The wall just keeps getting bigger.

Two years ago, I made a painful decision to move out. We did this amicably. I stayed in town and we saw each other every day. It was the hardest thing I ever had to do. My children were fairly young at the time, but it devastated them and this is what broke me. During this separation, my husband and I talked more than we had in the last eight years...you know.... stuff like our needs...what makes us happy and sad...whatever. Against the advice of my counselor I went back to my family. Guess what? Things have reverted to what it was like before...I know it takes two people to make it work...but doesn't the love and respect have to be there? How can two people share the same house and yet be so out of touch with each other? Should it always be the same person trying? I'm so mentally exhausted and hurt.

I want to add my husband and I haven't been intimate for the last 5 years. After our first child it was 2 years before we were intimate, and then our second child came and this time it was 3 years. I couldn't handle it...I "jumped ship"(as you would say). I am so very tired. More than anything I want my children to see what a loving relationship should be like...my husband thinks things are "okay" and that things will get better...how will they? He won't come to counseling. He just wants "us" to work it out. What do you think? Is it possible? I am going to a counselor...I need to.... I just can't keep it together without talking to someone.

Marriage isn't supposed to be like this...is it? I love my children. I can't leave again. I just don't know what to do.

Larry responds:
Thanks for your email.

As noted, it takes two people to marry but only one to divide the family in half. Ask your husband if he wants to be a part of an entire family or half a family? As I have heard from my clients, it takes two people to keep a marriage together. Two active people, not just one.

Try getting your husband to read the book. You read it too. Use some of the tips to keep it together if you can.

All the best.

Thanks for the email.
Larry

Wife Learns Meaning of Joint Ownership Too Late
Hi Larry:

Greetings from Fort Worth

Your book is a real eye opener. I never understood what joint ownership meant till I read your book. I thought when I had things in joint names with my husband I owned half and could do with it as I please. I never realized that I couldn't leave my half of the house to my only child from my first marriage. Why didn't my attorney tell me about this??? I read with interest your chapter on protecting yourself. It is too late for me but I am going to make sure my son gets the straight goods from your book before he gets married. I am sure many married couples do the exact opposite of what you recommend just because they don't know any better.

Thanks for writing it.

Son 22 +Woman 49 = Trouble
Dear Larry:

Great job on the radio. I was in my car and sat in the driveway when I got home to listen to the whole show. I've ordered your book — can't wait to get it. It's going on my coffee table.

My son, who is now 22, met a woman at the golf course during one summer he was working as a caddie. The problem is she is 49 and has 3 kids, one of which is his age and my son wants to marry this woman. He inherited a great deal of money from his grandmother. I'm worried this woman thinks she has found a young stud with money.

You should be commended for writing this book. I ordered it

because it is my only hope to get through to my son. You touched upon a few legal tips on the show. It sounds like your book will be the cold shower he needs right now.

You Wanted Them Now They're Yours

Dear Larry:
Great show. I am a regular viewer of your call in TV segment.

I always listen to your words of relationship wisdom. Now I hope you will listen to me. Put this in your next book! It is about a warning sign during the engagement period.

When I first met my now ex-wife we discussed the issue of children. She didn't want any kids. I did. I come from a big family. I always felt I would be able to change her mind. Once we got married and our friends started to have children her biological alarm clock went off. So we had kids. We have four. Last year something happened. I got a call from my wife in New Mexico telling me the business trip she went on was not a business trip but a one way ticket with her boss. They both decided life was too short to have to bother with kids. Her reply to me after I asked her why she had the kids was, "you wanted them, now they are yours." Is there an organization you are aware of for single dad's whose wives have abandoned their kids?

Short Engagement Too Tough For
Line Backer To Tackle

Dear Larry:
My marriage was anything but a fairy tale. When I met Jim at Ohio State he was everything I dreamed for in a man. Jim was 6 feet 4 inches, 250 pounds and a line backer. He could tackle the best of them. He also had a tender side. Jim played the violin. Jim was my

"prince charming."

I will never forget the first Christmas I took Jim back to meet my parents. My dad was impressed with his strong and secure handshake. Dad judged all my suitors by the way they shook his hand. My mother loved Jim too. Mom loved the fact Jim could talk to dad about football and to her about classical music.

After dating Jim for 3 months I made my mind up I was going to be his wife and he would be the father of my children.

Jim didn't want to get married at first. He believed marriage was a life long commitment and the engagement period should be long enough to really get to know one another. I, on the other hand, was in love and with my parent's approval I was determined to marry him right away.

What a mistake!

After we got married, Jim never made it professionally in football. That was his life long dream. He blamed me for stifling his career because our courting distracted his career chances. He held this against me ever since. In fact, when he came home one night drunk, Jim showed his true colors. He took his trophies and my grandmother's china and smashed it all. Well, you can imagine we are no longer married. If only I had had your book, maybe my life would have been different.

The Law Is an "Ass"

Hey Larry: I read your article in the newspaper. You were talking about your stories and you suggested we write to you about our stories.

Here is mine:

I was married for 19-H years to a woman I thought I knew. We raised 3 wonderful children together who are now aged 14, 16, and

19 and had what I thought was a wonderful life and a bright future. There was one major issue though, my wife suffered from manic depression and I spent over 4 years going to psychiatrists with her to try to help her deal with and get through this illness.

My life and my children's lives were absolute hell for 4 years, but we stayed strong and were always there for her during the dark and very difficult times, hoping we could get through it and look ahead to better days. She had threatened suicide more than once and had been hospitalized on 3 separate occasions. Two years ago I discovered my wife was having an affair with an old high school boyfriend. She was supposed to come to my brother's wedding with my children and I, but opted out saying she wasn't feeling up to going. I discovered the next day she had spent the night in a hotel room with this guy. I told her the marriage was over and she tried to kill herself in our home, with the children there. I called 911 and she was taken to hospital. Well, the marriage is over, and I have sole custody of my three wonderful children, but here's the hurt...She hired a piranha of a lawyer and went after everything she could. She ended up with over half our possessions, half the savings (retirement funds, pensions etc.) that amounted to over $100,000.00. She sued me for spousal support to the tune of $4,000 a month and had the divorce agreement stipulate she would have no responsibility for the children's well being.

She has effectively stolen my children's future and doesn't seem to care, she tells me that she deserves the money and doesn't feel a bit guilty about taking from the children's needs.

She took an apartment but doesn't live there.

She effectively lives with her boyfriend but as long as she keeps the address, she is not living common-law, and therefore can continue to collect her $4,000 a month.

My daughter starts university this fall and I will be hard pressed to pay.... the $4,000 would certainly help. Isn't it unfair an adulterous spouse can do so much wrong, hurt so many people, and still continue to inflict damage for years after?

I have spoken to many people about the unfairness of having to pay spousal support when I have sole custody of my children.

Thankfully my children are very well adjusted and are much happier without the constant pain in their lives and I am in a very wonderful, healthy, happy, loving relationship with a woman who I love very much.

I thought you would find my story of interest.

Take care.

What Comes Around Goes Around With a Cheater

Dear Larry:

I read about you in the newspaper. Wow! Great idea for a book. Finally a common sense approach to the issue of relationships. Not some academic who has never been married before and learned everything from a book.

You know the story, you called "I can't weight" about the fitness trainer who cheated with his married clients. I got a better one for you. Listen to my story.

Please feel free to pass this story on. Call it "meet the cheat."

I met my ex-wife at a wedding. She was sitting at the same table with me with her now ex-husband. What an amazing evening that was. We talked for hours. She danced a few times with her ex, but I ended up dancing with her most of the evening because her ex had a sore back and had to leave the wedding early to go home to bed. About half an hour after he left, she whispered in my ear we should leave the wedding and go for coffee. We did, but I never expected coffee in a motel room with her.

The next day she called me and told me she wanted to see me again and that she didn't love her husband anymore. Well, I suspected the night before but never thought our fling would turn into a full-fledged romance. After a year of secretly meeting, we ended up getting married.

For the first five years everything went well until she convinced me we should buy a new house. During the construction, I was away on business and she insisted on being the general contractor. I must say she did a great job. All the trades told me how 'great she was' but I never took those comments literally until I started getting hang up calls 5 years later. I traced the numbers and discovered that it was the plumber, the electrician and drywall man. When I called them back, they told me they were just checking with Joan (my wife) to see if everything was OK. I'm in the marketing business but this is taking keeping in touch with your customers too far. When I confronted Joan with my suspicions she admitted to me she was having affairs with them all and blamed my job. My response to her was, I should have known — 'once a cheat always a cheat.'

Larry, pass this on to anyone who is thinking about hooking up with a cheater.

Words of Wisdom

Good job Larry, I am on my second marriage and believe that we must educate today's young people about love and relationships.

Step-son Becomes The "Devil in Disguise"

Larry:

Great name for a website. Thank you for providing a forum so that I can interact with others. I would like to hear from others who are in a similar situation to mine. Help. I married a great gal but her child is the devil in disguise. Boy, was he well behaved before we got married. I never heard a peep out of him. His mother nicknamed him "Dennis the menace."

Until we got married I never knew about the problems he was having in school with his teachers and other students. I never knew that he had been expelled for slashing a teacher's tires and that he had been banned from a local mall for vandalism. After we got married and I got a call from his school principal that the video camera had caught him vandalizing the school, I realized that my stepson and his mother had duped me.

My advice, Larry, tell the world to investigate BEFORE you marry someone with kids. My life is now filled with stress and unhappiness.

You Are Not Alone

Hello Larry:

I too had dreams of a happy house and I am about to be a former spouse.

Your chapter on separation helped me because I realize I am not alone. The way you described your separation is what I am living through today. I have lost 30 pounds, don't sleep and live with my parents again. I am embarrassed to see my friends and don't see my kids. Boy did I get cheated.

If my ex-wife had read your book before she decided to dump me maybe she would have considered an amicable way of ending our relationship.

Conclusion

Throughout this book I have discussed relationships, from dating to re-marriage. I have written about my own personal experiences and those of some of my clients. This book touches upon many of the practical, financial and legal issues that may arise during a relationship. I wrote this book because I want to tell it like it is.

I will always remember one elderly couple, in particular, who visited me to draw up their wills. They had been married for over 60 years. They appeared to be very much in love and their happiness intrigued me. They seemed to be a throwback to another time. They told me being happily married was like having sunshine in their lives every day. I told them I was writing a book about relationships. As they sat across from me, they spoke to me about their lives. They told me about their children, grandchildren, great grandchildren and about the 60th wedding anniversary party their children had just made for them. I couldn't help but wonder, why did it work out for them and not others? In light of their successful marriage, I asked if they had anything they could add to this book. They told me the secret to their relationship was that they started off as friends and over the years became the best of friends. This, they stressed, was the secret to any long term relationship. In fact, they left me with an interesting thought about marriage that I would like to share with you. They told me anyone thinking about taking the final step toward marriage should ask this question — "If the person you are thinking of marrying would be of the same sex as you, would you call this person your BEST friend?" If the answer is "no," something is wrong. Re-evaluate the relationship before it is too late.